PRAISE FOR

WITHOUT THE MASK

"As an elite student athlete at BYU, Charlie inspired millions and gained national attention as Cosmo the Cougar. Now, without the mask, Charlie inspires all of us to reexamine the way we view God's LGBTQ children. He bravely uses his life experience and spiritual maturity to teach important truths about eternal identity applicable to all. This book proves that Charlie is not only one of the greatest mascots of all time, but also a gifted writer, a positive role model, and a devoted disciple of Jesus Christ. It is sure to be a game changer."

—**STEVE YOUNG,** ESPN NFL
Pro Football Hall of Far

"Charlie provides perfect insight into the co
teens feel when they are realizing they are different and wondering how they will mesh their identity and faith. He beautifully weaves his life experiences with his connection to the Savior, knowing that he was created for a divine purpose, and gives hope to others that they can live as both LGBTQ people and members of their faith community. This book gives me hope that other kids like my son will now have an environment of understanding and kindness in their place of worship."

—**ALYSON PAUL DEUSSEN,** mother of Stockton Powers, who came out as gay at the age of 13 and died by suicide at the age of 17 in June 2016

"When I first met Charlie, he shared with me what he then saw as an irreconcilable conflict between his orientation and his long-held faith. Try as I might, I was unable to answer his questions, even to my own satisfaction. Until I read this very inspiring book,

I didn't fully understand the depth and breadth of his struggle, or the effort he has put into reconciling these two seemingly opposing forces. Charlie's insights have given me a better understanding of the far-reaching and infinite healing power of Christ's Atonement, as well as the simple truth that we are each a beloved child of perfect, loving Heavenly Parents. This book can assist anyone who is struggling with any gospel principle, any doubt, any disappointment, any seemingly overwhelming challenge."

—**BRYANT FOULGER,** bishop,
Washington D.C. 2nd Ward (YSA)

"For years I felt alone on a path that led to destruction with no hope. I began to push others away to hide what I was going through. I felt alone in my struggle to understand my sexuality and how it played a role in my eternal identity. When I heard Charlie Bird's testimony, something changed. I now have courage and hope for what's to come. Charlie is not telling you how to live; he is teaching us a method to find the purpose of our life through the Atonement of Christ. This book offers guidance to understand not only the struggles that LGBTQ+ people go through, but what we have to offer."

—**18-YEAR-OLD MALE,** name withheld

WITHOUT THE MASK

CHARLIE BIRD

COMING OUT AND COMING INTO GOD'S LIGHT

Dedicated to fourteen-year-old me:

You are what you always imagined you could be.

Visit us at deseretbook.com

Library of Congress Cataloging-in-Publication Data

Names: Bird, Charlie, 1993– author.
Title: Without the mask : coming out and coming into God's light / Charlie Bird.
Description: Salt Lake City : Deseret Book, [2020] | Includes bibliographical references. | Summary: "A former Brigham Young University mascot "Cosmo the Cougar," Charlie Bird, details his coming out as gay as a member of The Church of Jesus Christ of Latter-day Saints"—Provided by publisher.
Identifiers: LCCN 2020015165 | ISBN 9781629727844 (trade paperback)
Subjects: LCSH: Bird, Charlie, 1993– | Mormon gays—Biography. | Homosexuality—Religious aspects—The Church of Jesus Christ of Latter-day Saints. | Homosexuality—Religious aspects—Mormon Church. | LCGFT: Biographies.
Classification: LCC BX8643.H65 B57 2020 | DDC 289.3092 [B]—dc23
LC record available at https://lccn.loc.gov/2020015165

Printed in the United States of America
LSC Communications, Crawfordsville, IN

10 9 8 7 6 5 4 3 2 1

TABLE OF CONTENTS

LETTER TO THE READER

DEAR READER,

I aim to write the book I wish I would have had when I was fourteen—when I was confused, scared, and felt entirely unlovable. I want to write the book I needed when I was eighteen, when I felt defeated, broken, and completely alone. I want to write the book I wish I had when I was twenty-one, when the only future I could see was bleak and hopeless, and the book I searched for when I was twenty-four, when I saw few role models and felt I was the only person in the world walking the largely uncharted territory of being openly gay and active in my church.

I want to write a book that might help a dad better understand his son, or give peace to a mother who has been crying herself to sleep at night. I want to write a book for the youth leader who isn't sure how to create a safe space for LGBTQ youth while still teaching true gospel principles, and for the bishop who doesn't know how to support families that are day by day breaking apart. I hope reading my experiences will spark healing, bridge gaps of understanding, and inspire hope.

I pray that for someone, this will be the book I never had.

Sincerely,

CHARLIE BIRD

BEFORE YOU BEGIN

WITHOUT THE MASK alternates between memoir and teaching chapters. Memoir chapters tell stories of important events in my journey to understand who I am and how I've reconciled faith with sexual orientation. They give glimpses into challenges I have faced with my identity, growth I have experienced, and how I have been able to maintain healthy relationships with my family, my church, and my faith. Teaching chapters use my experiences and perspective to teach overarching truths I've learned about life, identity, and my relationship with God. Chapters and stories are organized by common themes, not chronological order.

The LGBTQ community is built of diverse souls with varied experiences. While I might be able to represent a small facet of this community, my views and experiences cannot speak for everyone. I have done my best to outline only my own, personal experiences as a gay member of The Church of Jesus Christ of Latter-day Saints. I recognize the privilege that has allowed me to share my story on a wider platform, and hope by doing so I can make room for others who might not have the same opportunities or resources I have been blessed with.

Before I begin, I would like to explain to readers how I identify, and why:

I label myself first and foremost as a Child of God. My divine identity as a son of Heavenly Parents influences everything that I am. I also identify as a member of The Church of Jesus Christ of Latter-day Saints. I value my membership in the Lord's Church, along with the sacred covenants I have made.

Life often requires me to use additional labels to help communicate important information about myself. I have qualities that the world connects to an array of terms, including *gay*, *sexual orientation*, *same-sex attraction*, *sexual identity*, *LGBTQ*, etc. Throughout my life, I have used various terms to convey my orientation, and I use many of them throughout this book.

Initially, I felt most comfortable describing myself as "having feelings of same-sex attraction" (commonly referred to as "SSA"). Many members of The Church of Jesus Christ of Latter-day Saints identify this way. While this term initially made my feelings seem safer and more manageable, I began to notice that for me, it made same-gender attraction feel like a temporary condition, or a problem that was constantly chasing me. I also noticed that, outside of a church setting, the phrase was seldom used and the acronym largely unknown.

I now feel most comfortable identifying as "gay." While I don't like the stigma that sometimes comes with the label, I do like that it is the only widely accepted term that implies orientation without being solely focused on sex or sexual attraction. It is important to me that the way I describe myself conveys something more than just physical attraction. "Gay" feels more representative of the essence of who I am—how I interact with others, the way I perceive the world, unique aspects of my personality, *and* my romantic attraction. When I began labeling myself as gay, I started putting less emphasis on my sexual orientation and more emphasis on all parts of who I am. This helped me feel happier and closer to God.

Words are placeholders for meaning, and sometimes they mean different things to different people. I ask all readers to be mindful that it is inappropriate to make assumptions about someone's actions or beliefs based solely on a label. If you have questions as to how someone identifies or what their label means to them, my advice would be to express a sincere desire to understand, then simply ask.

PROLOGUE

LIGHTS BLARED high above me as I eagerly waited for my cue. The dance team took their place at the center of the end zone, and before I knew it, the heavy beat of the music pounded through the stadium speakers. *Go time.* I fixated my line of vision directly on a midfield marker at the front of their formation, then ran out onto the field. Once there, I turned toward the crowd and lifted my arms to dance.

The sound was instant and deafening. It pierced right through the padding and fur that covered my ears. I couldn't see much through the mask, but I could feel the electric energy of the crowd: 60,000 people, all cheering for me. The intensity heightened my senses and pumped adrenaline through my veins. Any nervousness was immediately shaken off by my movements. Even with the considerable heat, weight, and restriction of the mascot suit, I brimmed with energy and confidence.

The next sixty seconds were a blurry mix of music, movement, heat, and noise. I threw my body into a flip and landed in a crouched position, perfectly in sync with the last beat of the music. The stadium erupted. I stood slowly and lifted my pointer finger into the sky. I felt invincible.

By the time I made it back to the student section, I had zero control over my body. I was pulled up into the crowd by a mass of screaming fans. They lifted me high above their heads and surfed me over the crowd. My logical side told me it was dangerous, but I trusted them. Their unified chant echoed through Utah Valley: "Cosmo! Cosmo! Cosmo!"

Feeling that valuable, that loved, was surreal.

For lack of adequate words to describe the experience: being Cosmo the Cougar, the mascot at Brigham Young University, was—seriously—so, so cool.

One day, while I was taking pictures with fans during a home football game, a little boy excitedly ran up to me and asked if I would autograph his football. I scribbled Cosmo's signature with a black Sharpie, then we passed it back and forth around the concession area. Before he left, he asked his parents to come over and take a picture of us together.

"He wants to be just like you when he grows up, Cosmo!" said his dad with a smile as he took the picture.

"All he wanted for his birthday was a poster of you," added his mom with a laugh. "Thanks for being such a good role model for our little boy."

I reached down to give the boy a hug, did a backflip, then gave each of his parents a high five before they walked off. The exchange was heartwarming, but as I headed back down to the field, I couldn't help but remember the night before. I had spent hours staring at the ceiling, kept awake by the haunting worry that I might never find true acceptance. Lately, it seemed the only time I felt belonging was when the real me was covered by the Cosmo mask.

I couldn't help but wonder, *If that family knew me without any masks, would they hate me? Would they let their son look up to me if they knew I was gay?*

It was sobering to think that the very community I represented was the one that made me feel most alienated. When I suited up and became the mascot, I had a place where I fit within my community. However, when the lights went down and the mask came off, I felt like an outsider.

1

THE ARCHITECT

I WAS ALMOST regretting my decision when I rounded the corner on 13th Street. Uneasiness moved through me with each step. *Was I really going to do this?*

The mid-morning sun beat above, blasting heat and harsh light through the wide city streets. Washington D.C. normally felt slow on Sundays, but today there was palpable energy. Vehicles that usually crowded the roads had been warded off by police tape and heavy orange cones. Cop cars, pedestrians, and traffic directors suggested a crowd was already forming a few blocks down.

An exceptional opportunity had brought me to D.C. for the summer. I was gearing up for my senior year at Brigham Young University, and had spent months looking for the right internship. It came by a last-minute marvel. Still an undergrad in the Marriott School of Business, I was thrilled to be granted an intern opening at the U.S. Department of Commerce. I said yes to the offer immediately and never looked back. I had now been working there for three weeks, and so far it was a perfect fit. I loved my job, and had my own office space in a beautiful neoclassical building. On weekends I got to run through the National Mall, roam Smithsonian Museums, and read on the steps of the Library of Congress.

I tried to reassure myself as I walked. I'd weighed all possible outcomes multiple times. Even if today was a disaster, if I played my cards right, there would be no major social consequences. I'd made a few friends at work, and had met a handful of people at church, but by all accounts I was a still a small fish in a very large pond. It didn't matter who saw me today, because nobody knew who I was. This felt like my one shot to make a big decision and still have an opportunity to back out if it didn't feel right.

I had felt a little weird about leaving sacrament meeting early. Once the bread and water were passed, I slipped out the side door as quietly as I could. Back at my dorm I had swapped my white collared shirt and slacks for my favorite Nike tee and a pair of khaki shorts. I looked down at my outfit of choice. What did people even wear to something like this? I didn't know. I hoped it wouldn't be too obvious that I had no idea what I was doing.

The night before, I had found a small group of members of The Church of Jesus Christ of Latter-day Saints on Facebook who planned to meet before D.C. Pride and walk together. I was incredulous when I first saw the e-flyer. *Did members of my church do that?* It seemed outlandish. I was almost sure the group was some sort of joke. If not, it would probably just be me and one other weird guy—maybe a crazy mom if I was lucky.

It wasn't ideal, but I was desperate.

Lately, the entire world seemed to revolve around the very thing I had been trying to escape. Politically and religiously, LGBTQ issues were more prevalent and pressing than ever before. Voices were loud and divided. Just two years earlier, I had watched protesters on the news march with handmade signs as the White House lit up in rainbow colors. Some loudly praised progress and equality, while others feared the moral fabric of society was unraveling before their very eyes. Now I was here, in the very same place, but the height of the conflict had moved from the streets to my soul.

It seemed there was no middle ground; to exist was to pick a side. Those who claimed "love wins" relentlessly attacked their religious friends and family on social media. Those who said "God is love" told their gay sons and daughters to not bother coming home for Christmas. Each side seemed equally convinced, equally zealous. There were voices everywhere. I had always been taught that truth was constant and objective, yet here I was, feeling hopelessly lost. I found myself trapped in a tornado of differing opinions, ideas, claims, and statistics.

I couldn't deny what I knew. God was alive and real, Jesus Christ was my Savior, and family relationships were divinely appointed and eternal. On the other hand, however, I couldn't deny what I felt. I was attracted to men, and no matter how hard I tried, that still hadn't changed.

Over the past year I'd been watching people. Most of the time I studied online, tucked safely behind the cover of a computer screen, but a few times I had timidly attended LDS/SSA support groups. Under the guise of curiosity or made-up school assignments, I listened to people's experiences. Many expressed an unshakable feeling of sorrow, while others came across wild and bitter to me. I met some people whose entire lives seemed to be a constant cycle of fear, anger, and sadness. From what I witnessed, a lot of people who loved the Church hated themselves, and many who loved themselves hated the Church. I wondered if there was a way for me to love both.

Before that, my approach had been less analytical. I had always known I was different from other guys, but it wasn't until

I was about fourteen that I figured out why. The realization that I was attracted to men brought with it a potent mix of emotions that crashed in on me all at once—anxiousness, excitement, longing, thrill, confusion, and heartbreak. In that moment, the childlike innocence of my youth suffered its first real fracture. On the surface I was still my bright, positive self, but from then on I lived with the painstaking weight of a confusing sexual orientation—a deep, troublesome undercurrent of fear.

As a member of The Church of Jesus Christ of Latter-day Saints in the rural Midwest, most everything I'd ever heard about "homosexuality" was coupled with a highly negative connotation. I wasn't sure why I felt attracted to men, but my life experience had taught me it was an embarrassing, shameful thing. At fourteen, I decided the best approach would be to pray, keep quiet, and just try to avoid my feelings. I hoped by doing so, they would eventually disappear.

But they never did. In the years that followed, I went into attack mode. I tried everything I could to rewire my brain, but to my disillusion, no amount of pamphlets, scriptures, fasting, prayer, or psychological exercises had any effect on the way I felt. I let extracurricular activities and volunteer projects consume my life as a purposeful distraction from facing who I was. Over time I conditioned myself to become completely homophobic, desperately trying to convince myself that I could run away. I hoped if I ran fast enough, my unwelcome feelings could never catch up to me.

Now I was twenty-three. I'd spent almost ten years clawing for a solution that seemed impossible. Sometimes I felt I was making progress, but most of the time I just felt my soul was being torn apart. I felt like a living dichotomy—a vortex of two parts that couldn't exist simultaneously. I wanted peace and happiness, but I didn't know how to find it, especially when each new day brought intense religious and social turmoil. Bishops told me to continue to fast, pray, and keep the faith; bloggers told me to release myself from the vice grip of organized religion. Everyone seemed to have a different idea of what happiness was. Even when people claimed to have answers, none of them seemed right for me.

Moments later I arrived at the bakery where the group had planned to meet, still unsure if I could actually get myself to go inside. Until recently I had avoided gay people at all costs. Honestly, it had been pretty easy. I grew up on a cattle ranch in southwest Missouri in a conservative town of just over 3,000 people. After graduating high school, I went straight to Brigham Young University, where I was surrounded by people of a similar background and faith. My only experience living outside of Missouri or Utah was when I lived in Southern California for two years, but as a full-time Church missionary, my association with gay people was limited, to say the least.

In D.C., however, there was no way to avoid it. Restaurants boasted rainbow flags, and other churches flaunted giant banners that said, "All are welcome." I was shocked to see gay couples in public, smiling, holding hands, and pushing strollers. I had gay colleagues at work and gay floormates in my dorms. Growing up, I'd solidified in my mind there was nothing worse than accepting someone with a "gay lifestyle," yet here I was, surrounded by gay people, and their lifestyles seemed pretty much like everyone else's. I was immersed in one of the most LGBTQ-affirming cities in the world, and no one seemed as dangerous or scary as I'd imagined. On the contrary, many of them were kind, smart, and creative.

Were gay people really that bad? Was I one of them?

For better or for worse, my long journey had taken me here, to the front door of a bakery on 13th Street. Nothing had worked in the past, and it was time to try a new approach. With a final nod, I pulled the metal door handle and made my way through the entrance.

Sure enough, at the back of the small shop there was a crowd wielding homemade signs, everything from "God loves all His children" to "You don't have to push a handcart to be a pioneer." There were a lot more people than I expected. Some were still in their Sunday best, while others donned hats and tank tops. I anxiously paced by the trash can while I mustered up the courage to go introduce myself.

"Hi. Is this the LDS Pride group?" I asked nervously.

"Yes! We're glad you found us," said a guy on the edge of the group. He was wearing a Nike shirt and shorts, just like me. I felt a little more at ease. We quickly exchanged names.

"What brings you here?" he asked.

"I'm Mormon . . ." I paused. "And I'm . . . gay . . ."

I had never said it out loud. Not in public. Not like that. My stomach twisted in knots. I wanted to run outside, jump in the nearest manhole, and disappear forever. I was crazy. What was I doing? Why had I come here?

"Congratulations! Me too," he replied with a laugh. "We're still waiting on a few more before we head over to the march. Come, sit down! I'll introduce you to everyone."

I had never dreamed I would ever participate in a Pride event. Rainbow flags made me uncomfortable. Seeing gay couples had always made me feel nervous and uneasy. And I wasn't proud of my same-sex attraction; I had always been completely ashamed of it. Yet, an hour later, I found myself holding up the "pioneer" sign and walking alongside a hodgepodge group of what I usually considered crazy, progressive believers. It felt bold, unfamiliar, and bizarre.

That evening I sat on the edge of the Capitol reflecting pool and watched the sunset. In the distance I could still see remnants of the Pride parade. Some people in bright colors were still dancing and laughing together, while others said goodbyes and hopped in taxis. I was proud of myself for stepping out of my comfort zone. I usually spent all my energy running away, but today I'd been courageous. Today, at the very least, I had tried to see things from a new perspective—that had to count for something, right?

As I watched the sun melt behind the Washington Monument, I got lost in my thoughts. I'd been trying to find answers for so long. I had read everything the Church had ever published about "homosexuality." I had combed blogs and general conference talks for years. I had asked ecclesiastical leaders, therapists, and now even strangers for advice. I'd even been to a gay pride parade. I'd looked into every path I could possibly find, but confusion and sadness still overwhelmed me. It was so hard to see how God could possibly have a place for me. I felt like His entire plan was set up just for me to fail.

Then, as I sat and pondered on the warm, sloped concrete, watching reflections of the fire-orange sun dance on the ripples in the water, a new thought entered my mind:

I had asked God to change my nature, but I had never asked for guidance on how to honor it.

Any prayers I had ever offered about my orientation were guarded and formal. I would spend hours apologizing for my existence, then beg God to change me. Each prayer was a desperate plea for the Lord to take away my feelings and make me straight. I'd always lived under the impression that God hated this part of me. I'd never considered that maybe there was a purpose behind it. I'd never asked if I should accept my orientation, or how to better understand it.

I wasn't sure if it was something I could ask; the thought had never even occurred to me until now. The whole topic was, and always had been, completely off-limits. When it came to same-gender attraction, I had always seen God as an intimidating authority figure rather than a loving Father. I worried asking my questions might make Him more disappointed in me than I figured He already was. Would He be insulted? Would He be upset?

But as I considered this new viewpoint, I thought of James 1:5, one of the first scriptures I had memorized as a child: "If any of you lack wisdom, let him ask of God, that giveth to all men liberally, and upbraideth not; and it shall be given him." Peace flooded my heart. I knew that if anyone needed wisdom, it was me. As I sat there by the reflecting pool, my soul opened to the possibility that I really could ask God, and I wouldn't offend Him with my questions. Without realizing, I found myself offering a sincere prayer of gratitude. I hadn't been grateful for my life in quite some time.

Maybe Heavenly Father has answers for me, I thought hopefully. *Maybe He can help me cut through all the noise.*

I determined to go to the source.

A few weeks later I stood outside the Washington D.C. Temple, looking up at the pristine, white building. I had always been fascinated by architecture and design. As charming as the brown scratchy walls and green polyester carpets in my local meetinghouse were, what really captivated me were temples. Temples were magical and mysterious, like big ivory castles. Each one was unique and beautiful. I used to fantasize about being head architect at Church headquarters, drawing ornate floor plans and creating stunning exteriors to adorn cities all over the world.

One year the *Friend* magazine had a "temples of the world" craft section. Each month for an entire year I cut out the pictures, carefully glued them to cardstock paper, and made flash cards so I could memorize them. By December I could recognize and name every temple in the world at that time, all 108 of them. I made a list of my top-ten favorites, along with a goal to visit each one.

The Washington D.C. Temple was high on my list. I considered it one of the most beautiful of all. Its six-spire design mimicked the iconic Salt Lake Temple, but there was a unique grandeur and elegance to it that captivated me. I read about how the architect had used thinly sliced marble throughout the design, allowing a translucent glow of light to enter the building without the need for traditional windows. If that wasn't compelling enough, I also knew that on each end of the temple there were running panels of stained glass, seven stories high. For years I had dreamed of seeing the building and experiencing the innovative lighting techniques firsthand.

Now, when it was finally time to go inside, I felt like I was right back at the front door of the bakery before the Pride march. I paced back and forth, full of apprehension, almost regretting my decision. It was difficult to muster the courage to go in, but eventually I walked myself through the front door. Lately, the temple hadn't been a place of peace, revelation, or even beauty for me. It was just a stark reminder of all the ways I didn't fit in.

"Are you waiting for your sweetheart?" an elderly man dressed in white asked as I waited in the chapel for the session to start.

"No. I don't have one," I replied shortly.

"Ah. Well, don't you worry. A fine, good-looking young man

like you should have no problem finding a wife. I'm sure she will come along sooner than you think," he said with a wink, and he sauntered off.

He was the third person to ask about my "sweetheart" since I had entered the building just ten minutes before.

I had come to find answers, but all I was finding was anxiety. I was accustomed to feeling a little anxious and somewhat out of place in the temple, but today it was worse than ever before. Throughout the session I caught myself staring at the door, wondering how long I could override my body screaming at me to leave. I felt like I didn't belong there. I felt like I didn't belong anywhere—I was gay. Not even the thinly cut marble walls could keep me calm. My desire to get the answer I was seeking was the only thing that kept me in my chair.

Time after time I tried to pray, but nothing happened. I couldn't connect. I left the celestial room feeling angrier and more confused than ever. I was supposed to get answers today. I had been fasting, praying, and preparing for this moment for weeks. I was supposed to find peace, but I got nothing. Maybe this was off-limits, or maybe God just didn't care.

I didn't have any other plans, and I obviously wasn't going to have the life-changing spiritual experience I was hoping for, so I began aimlessly walking up and down a spiral staircase. I studied the way the soft light of the morning sun came through the thin marble walls. I got distracted by the stained glass; it really was stunning. Bright shades of blue, green, and purple cast iridescent light on the walls behind me. I walked up and down the stairs, lost in a kaleidoscope of color.

When I came to a quiet landing I paused. Soft, cream-colored carpet spilled from the staircase into a hallway in front of me. It felt different there. It felt calm, welcoming, and sacred.

I didn't have to pretend to be something I wasn't; I was just me.

I felt safe.

I quietly slipped from the landing to a secluded spot where the marble walls cast a soft glow on the carpet. I felt small compared to the grandeur of the building that surrounded me. I stood there for a while, perfectly still, letting myself be completely present in the moment. Soon, my apprehension and nervousness withdrew and were replaced by calm, hopeful anticipation.

I closed my eyes and began to pray.

"Heavenly Father," I said out loud, "I've tried so hard to do everything right. I don't understand . . ."

I shared my frustrations. I threw out the staged formalities of my old prayers and told God about my confusion and the heaviness of my situation. I explained how the years I had spent hating gay people hadn't changed me, but only caused me to hate myself. I begged Him to tell me why I felt like I couldn't find any answers, and why the Atonement seemed to work for everyone else but me. I explained how nothing I tried felt successful, and how emotionally exhausted I was from running away.

When I finished venting, I told Heavenly Father how I had felt at the Capitol reflecting pool a few weeks prior. I prayed that, if my sexual orientation really never would change, I could at least come to understand why it was part of me. I asked Heavenly Father if divine love was really all-encompassing, and if He could love and accept me despite the complete wreck I felt that I was. I asked God if He had a place for me, and if He did, to please show me where.

"Guide me, Lord. Please," I begged. "Give me answers."

I remained there alone, silent tears streaming down my face.

Then, I heard a voice enter my mind, as clear as if someone else had been in the room with me.

"I love you. I created you."

They were simple words, but they transformed me. I realized that God didn't hate me. He wasn't ashamed of who I was. He hadn't messed up when He made me. My dark, tired soul instantly filled with light. I felt the arms of redeeming love reach deep into my heart, pulling me from the abyss where I had been living.

The insight was the green light I needed to ask deeper questions, and I asked the rest of what had been weighing on my soul. As I meditated and prayed, I received deeply personal answers concerning the nature of my orientation and its role in my personal spiritual progression. Answers came easily, as if they had been there for a while, and God had simply been waiting for me to ask.

I felt closer to my Heavenly Parents as I sought heavenly guidance concerning who I am. I realized that They knew my soul and had a perfect knowledge of who I was. Trying to be somebody else had only put distance between us. The Spirit testified to me that I should no longer punish myself, run away, or feel ashamed: My Heavenly Parents loved me, and I should extend love to myself as well.

As I continued to pour out my heart, I had a remarkable impression that in the pre-earth life I had understood what I would face coming into the world and had been eager to take it on. Being born at this specific time, when I would be forced to wrestle with difficult questions of faith, identity, and sexuality, wasn't happenstance. There had been no coincidence, no mistake.

Since childhood I had been taught that God was the architect of my soul—an all-knowing, eternal Father who had created me by divine design. Now, I finally felt it was true. As I came to a better understanding of my relationship with Him, I began to see my peculiarity from an entirely new perspective.

This sudden paradigm shift in how I viewed myself brought

me a deeper understanding of my Savior. For years I had been pleading for the Lord to change me—to "fix" me. I had faith in the healing power of Jesus Christ, and I had thought changing my orientation was the only way to be whole. Here, however, as I communed with the Lord in His holy house, I finally understood: Christ's Atonement wasn't there to alter my orientation; it was there to heal my heart. Jesus suffered and subjected Himself to my pain so He could lift me from the heavy burdens of shame, hatred, and confusion I carried.

I felt a pull to no longer hide who I am. The Spirit assured me I would find power in being vulnerable, and that sharing my testimony and experiences would spark connection. I resolved to prayerfully "come out" to friends and loved ones if I ever felt prompted.

I closed my prayer with faithful assurance that more answers and continued guidance would come in time. After voicing a quiet "amen" I remained still.

Was that real? I wondered.

I felt a soft rush of cool air brush against my face, coming down from a vent above. I noticed the wiry thread of the embroidered carpet beneath me. I felt my fingers intertwined against each other, and a key twisted in my left pocket, pressing against my leg.

It was real.

"I'm supposed to be this way," I thought out loud. My voice seemed to encompass the entire room.

I opened my eyes and looked out at the temple surrounding me. Everything was exactly the same as it had been before I had begun praying, but I was changed. I knew, without any doubt, I was the eternal son of a loving Father in Heaven. For the first time in my life, I fully believed there was a place for me in God's kingdom. I imagined myself in heaven, dancing and singing with the angels above. The moment was sweet beyond words—I had never imagined myself in heaven before.

The stained glass was even more beautiful as I made my way down the spiral staircase. I walked through the foyer and out the front doors feeling humbled by the light and knowledge I had received. I had been created intentionally, just like the temple behind me. As I stepped into the sun and took one last look at the dazzling building, my heart swelled with gratitude and new hope.

I was not deficient, flawed, or defective.

I wasn't unsalvageable or broken.

The Architect had a plan for me.

2

JESUS MADE FLOWERS

MY FIRST TASTE of performing on a football field came when I was about nine years old. My family was all-in when it came to high school sports, and our community involvement led me to secure a spot as "coach's assistant" for the high school team. I loved helping out and watching from the sidelines. Most of the time I just refilled waters or carried towels, but eventually I was given the highly coveted job of going to fetch the plastic football tee after kickoff. One cool October evening, after watching the cheer squad perform a halftime routine, I had a brilliant idea.

For the previous few weeks, I'd been obsessed with back handsprings. I had seen someone do one in my karate class, and since then it had been all I could think about. I practiced wherever I could—in the yard, on the trampoline, even in the living room. I was getting pretty good, so that night, instead of simply running to grab the tee, I decided to spice things up a little and do back handsprings across the field until I reached the center.

I felt like a certified superstar as I tumbled across the grass. I did a round-off, followed by three consecutive back handsprings—the most I had ever done. I was thrilled to hear cheers from the crowd as I picked up the little orange tee and ran it back to the sidelines. I was proud of myself, and I even got a paragraph written about me in a local newspaper that covered the game.

My fame and self-satisfaction were short-lived, however. At church the following Sunday, I was taunted by some of the kids my age. "Male cheerleaders are gay," I overheard. "He probably just wants to be the water boy so he can be around football guys." I wasn't sure what they meant, or why I was being teased. I did like being around the football guys—I felt important and cool when I helped out on the sidelines. I couldn't figure out why that was a bad thing, or why they tried to make me feel embarrassed for doing something I thought was cool. All I really knew was that a lot of the things I did seemed to be considered girly, and guys who did girly things were called gay.

Throughout middle school I became extremely self-conscious of the way I sat, how I stood, and words I used. I watched other people who didn't get made fun of and tried to be exactly like them. Over time, I developed a list of "rules" to follow in order to fit in better with other guys around me. *Don't cross your legs*, I would remind myself. *People will think you're gay.* I learned to highlight my stereotypically masculine interests, such as hiking or camping, and downplay other things, like how much I loved dance and fantasy fiction novels.

There were some people I could relax around. For the most part, my family let me be authentic without too much judgment. I felt especially comfortable around my little sister Hannah, whose natural personality broke down my walls. I could always be my true self around her. We would have dance-offs before bed, watch romantic comedies, and throw impromptu fashion shows, and I never worried what she thought about me.

Society, however, taught me from a young age that femininity was gay, and gay was bad. I constantly worried about what everyone else thought of me. As I got older, I frequently felt like an outsider, especially in all-guy groups.

There was a time when I felt so out of place that I stopped going to Young Men classes at church. On the southwest corner of our building there was a small, seldom-used room. It could only fit a few chairs, was awkwardly shaped, and the chalkboard didn't erase well. When I realized the room was empty, I started hiding in it instead of going to class.

One Sunday my older sister Janine followed me to figure out where I had been hiding. I was the kind of kid who memorized scriptures for fun and never missed a day of early-morning seminary. Skipping class wasn't my usual style.

"Charlie? What are you doing in here? Why aren't you in class?" she asked.

I had been sitting on the floor playing with my phone case. I didn't say anything. I didn't want to talk to anyone, but she sat with me for a while and told me about what she had learned in Sunday School.

"Charlie, what's up?" she finally asked after a few minutes of failing to engage me in the conversation. Her voice was kind and free of judgment. "You can talk to me," she said.

I tried to fight it, but I trusted her and needed to talk.

"I'm a freak, Janine."

"What do you mean?" she asked, trying to mask the concern in her voice.

"I don't fit in. I'm not like other guys," I broke.

"How?"

"I've never been like other guys. They like contact sports, and . . . fighting, and I . . ."

"You play a ton of sports," she countered, sounding a little confused. "And you're good. Do you not think you're athletic enough?"

"I love sports, but not cool ones. I like cross-country and cheerleading. I like gymnastics and dance. I mean, I played basketball, but mostly just because everyone else does. It's not like it was a huge surprise when I got cut from the team . . ." I trailed off. "It's not about sports, though—it's . . . it's everything about me," I rushed.

"What do you mean?"

I told her how I got made fun of for my "girly" handwriting and for being in show choir. I explained how I felt the need to pretend like I was interested in things just so people wouldn't pick on me. I told her how I was embarrassed of my creativity and my love for art, dancing, and decorating. I told her how I wanted to try out for the cheer squad, but I was afraid I would be mocked if I did.

"I can't go to Young Men, Janine. I'm not a real man. I don't belong there."

"You think you are less of a man just because some seventeen-year-old bullies say you're too feminine?" she asked.

"Well, they're right," I replied.

Janine paused and thought for a moment.

"Charlie—Jesus made flowers," she said.

"What?"

"Think about the Creation—Jesus made flowers," she repeated. "Jesus Christ, the most perfect man that has ever lived, made flowers." Tears began to form in the corners of her eyes. "He is creative like you, Charlie. He has a sincere love of beauty, and an affinity for design. He is compassionate and kind and emotional, just like you are."

My soul felt lighter as she spoke.

"Being a man has nothing to do with gender stereotypes, Charlie. All these things that you are embarrassed of—they make you more like Jesus. The very qualities you are ashamed of are, in fact, innate Christlike characteristics."

Janine explained to me how femininity is divine. She used Jesus's creation of—and biblical references to—flowers as an example to help me understand that my interests and personality were nothing to hide. She explained that masculinity had nothing to do with what sports I played, what kind of books I read, or how big I was. Being a real man was about how I used my time and talents to serve others. She taught me that, rather than define my characteristic traits as exclusively feminine or masculine, I should define them by whether or not they were Christlike.

I learned an important lesson that day, one that would change the way I viewed myself. Before that moment, I had never considered how many of the Savior's qualities are, in our world today, considered feminine. Jesus is a perfect example of patience, empathy, understanding, and sensitivity. He is nurturing, gentle, accommodating, and emotional. He is compassionate, kind, and conscious of others. In His great and ultimate atoning sacrifice, the Savior proved to be the epitome of humility and vulnerability, both viewed as stereotypically feminine by modern society.

Scripture often refers to Christ or Christlike attributes in the female form. Throughout His earthly ministry, the Savior was known to have taken on many feminine and motherly roles. He prepared food for multitudes, washed and anointed others with oils, and suffered children to come unto Him. Christ's role as a teacher is often one that women fill, both in the home and in society. Even the emblems of the holy sacrament, which represent Christ's spiritual sustenance of the world through His flesh and blood, are an archetype of a mother sustaining the life of an unborn child through her own flesh and blood.

In many instances, Christ refers to His own characteristics in the female form. In Isaiah 66:13, the pre-earthly Messiah told Israel, "As one whom his mother comforteth, so will I comfort you." 3 Nephi tells us that when He was among the Nephites, Jesus repeated a maternal phrase originally recorded in Matthew four consecutive times: "How oft would I have gathered you as a hen gathereth her chickens under her wings" (3 Nephi 10:5). These scriptural examples make a direct comparison of the Savior of the world to a female mother figure.

Alma prophesied that Christ would "go forth, suffering pains and afflictions and temptations of every kind" and "take upon him the pains and the sicknesses of his people." He also said Jesus would take upon Himself everyone's infirmities, "that his bowels may be filled with mercy, according to the flesh, that he may know according to the flesh how to succor his people" (Alma 7:11–12). The Savior fulfilled this prophecy when He atoned for humankind in the Garden of Gethsemane, died on the cross, and rose again on the third day as the resurrected Lord.

As Christ ministered among the Nephites, He invited them to come forth one by one and touch Him, that they might know of a surety that He was "God of the whole earth" (3 Nephi 11:14). In the same way that each Nephite felt the wound marks in His hands, feet, and side individually, Christ felt our wounds individually. He descended below all to suffer our pains, heartaches, and experiences according to the flesh. This infinite Atonement allows Him to understand *all* of us—women, men, children, and anyone in between. He has a perfect knowledge of everyone's life situation, regardless of gender, race, or identity. He knows how to succor each one of His people, as a mother knows intuitively how to succor and care for a child.

Because of His infinite Atonement, Jesus Christ understands how it feels to be me. He knows what it's like to be a man with many innate feminine characteristics. He understands how social norms, stereotypes, and gender roles have affected me throughout my life. He knows my personality and can teach me how to use it to be a better disciple. Accessing the enabling power of Christ has taught me to not see my stereotypically feminine traits as "less than" or "embarrassing." In fact, qualities that some label as "girly" or "gay" frequently allow me to connect with others and love as the Savior loved.

The first time I truly let myself be "gay" was while serving as a missionary. Initially, I didn't know if same-sex attraction would prevent me from successfully serving. I was scared of not being able to control my feelings and worried I wouldn't connect well with companions and other missionaries. Even worse, I was terrified that somehow I would "out" myself and be sent home early. Though valid at the time, all of these fears, and many more, dissipated as soon as I received a priesthood blessing and was set apart for the work.

As I served, I hardly thought about attraction, men, or relationships at all. Instead, I was focused on perfecting my Spanish and teaching people about Christ. The mantle of my sacred calling allowed me to operate at a level free from romantic distraction and free from fear of what other people thought about me. I had a clear purpose and didn't have much time to think about anything other than how my companion and I were going to fit a service project in between scheduled teaching appointments. When I wore my missionary name tag, I wasn't seen as masculine or feminine, gay or straight—I was just seen as Elder Bird.

Without the stress and pressure of constantly running from who I was, for the first time ever I allowed myself to live free and authentically. I began to embrace, and even promote, parts of my personality that I had rarely shown before. Each tendency or trait that I had previously stifled, for fear of being perceived as effeminate, I now acted on. I soon noticed I developed deeper relationships and felt happiest when I let the Spirit work through my whole self.

Before my mission I worked at a grocery store bakery as a cake decorator. I love decorating cakes, and have a natural gift for it, but every time someone I knew came into the bakery I slunk behind the counter, wrestled on my jacket, and snuck away to the back freezer to hide. I didn't want anyone at school to know that my job was making buttercream roses in an apron.

On my mission, however, I let members of local congregations know that I was a professionally trained cake decorator. I used my skills to bless people's lives. I made cakes for people who had upcoming weddings or anniversary parties but didn't have the funds to order custom-made designs. One time I even saved an event when the cake fell and was destroyed just ten minutes before the party was to start. I slapped on a #12 tip and cranked out a dozen icing roses before anyone could even bat an eye.

I embraced other talents I had previously hidden as well. Rather than being embarrassed of my handwriting, I made colorful, elaborate thank-you and birthday cards for members of the congregation to help them feel valued and seen. I potted plants and decorated apartments for homesick missionaries to help them feel more welcome and at ease. I played the piano for the church choir, and did flips and cheer routines to entertain kids at church gatherings.

As I allowed myself to be authentic without fear of being

labeled or bullied for being "gay," my experiences echoed what Janine had said about the Savior and femininity. When I fully embraced who I was, I was able to better help bring people to Christ. My feminine traits helped me gain the trust of those around me, and I felt an increased sense of purpose and belonging as I used my unique personality to serve others.

I became comfortable letting my uninhibited self shine through, even when I was around other guys my age. I spent the summer of 2014 pedaling a bike around San Bernardino, California, in a white button-down, a double Windsor necktie, and black dress shoes. Life was a heavy rotation of sweaty scriptures, corn tortillas, and palm trees. Mornings consisted of studying the scriptures, reading in Spanish, and patching holes in bicycle tires. Afternoons were spent running from stray dogs, meeting with complete strangers, and teaching the restored gospel of Christ.

In late May, my companion and I met Arturo, a twenty-two-year-old from Mexico City. Our friend Douglas, who had recently moved to the U.S. from Costa Rica, started accompanying us to lessons at Arturo's house. In a few short weeks, the four of us became our own kind of dream team. We did service projects together, planned Church activities, visited widows, and jokingly made fun of each other's accents. On free days we grabbed tacos, went on hikes, and hit up cheap bowling alleys. I was completely myself, and they all liked me more for it. To Arturo, Douglas, and Elder Olsen, I wasn't gay, straight, or girly; I was just one of the boys.

One unforgettable July night, the four of us stood together in an empty baptismal font at the local church building. Elder Olsen's voice echoed off the tile walls as he explained to Douglas how to perform a baptism. Arturo took his position with an eager smile on his face, and I watched their reflection in the mirror above as Douglas practiced "submerging" Arturo through the empty air. The love and brotherhood in the small font were almost tangible. I realized I could be myself around other guys and still fit in. These mission experiences taught me that I connect more with others and become more like the Savior when I am true to who I am.

In the New Testament, the Savior commanded that all must "become as little children" (Matthew 18:3). Watching my nieces and nephews has helped me better understand this commandment. They are able to live so freely and honestly, without the fear of being labeled or judged. Once, when a sudden crack of thunder scared my little nephew, he said, "Mom, I'm scared. Will you hold me?" His innocence and sincerity were pure and untainted by the scrutiny of the world.

When I was a child, I too lived free from judgment regarding my personality and actions. I drew butterflies with pink markers, cried when I was sad, and did back handsprings on the football field instead of simply running out to retrieve the football tee. As I grew older, however, I felt like I had to change who I was in order to fit in. I hid certain qualities and lost the childlike purity of my true self, often leading me to feel isolated and uncomfortable.

I remember feeling too gay to be Cosmo on the first day of tryouts. After performing fairly well in a grueling physical test against athletes from across the country, I felt humiliated during one of the first rounds of skill-based assessments. One by one, participants were called up and asked to throw a ball at a target on the wall. Each of them threw the ball once, then sat back down on the sidelines. When it was my turn, I was asked to throw the ball over and over and over again. Out of the corner of my eye I saw the coach scribbling on a clipboard after each throw, making me increasingly paranoid. I could almost see his notes in my mind: "Looks gay—throws like a girl."

All week I had been looking forward to the skills assessment that would showcase my greatest asset: dance. However, when that section of tryouts finally came around, I looked out at the room full of strangers and remembered how embarrassed I had felt while throwing the ball. When it was my turn, I was so worried about looking "too gay" that I purposefully toned down my performance. I withheld my signature twists and body rolls, and instead tried to impersonate a more masculine, rugged version of myself. I did the bare minimum just to show that I had rhythm, then sat back down.

When tryouts were over, there was nothing to set me apart from the other prospects, and I didn't make the team. Instead, I spent the next few semesters as a "coach's assistant." I moved mats across campus, organized equipment, cleaned suits, and refilled water bottles in exchange for the opportunity to attend practices. Sometimes I got to fill in for smaller events that the real Cosmo couldn't make, but nothing but my work ethic really kept me around.

Even though I wasn't Cosmo, I enjoyed helping out. I felt useful, and I loved getting to see football games directly from the sidelines. I always watched closely when the Cougarettes performed during the first-quarter break. They were hip-hop perfection, with sharp lines and big hair-ography. As I watched, I wanted nothing more than to be out on the field with them. I often pictured myself in the cougar suit, posing at the head of their formation, waiting for my cue. I knew I had the talent to make it happen, even though nobody else did.

Eventually, I threw out my fear of being labeled as too feminine or too gay and started practicing. I watched dance videos and worked on choreography until I was sure that my hips and arms could move in sync with theirs. I presented my idea to the coaches, then held nothing back when I tried out to dance with the Cougarettes during their homecoming performance.

It took fifteen years, but the same boy that once got ridiculed for performing on a football field finally found the courage to do it again. This time, however, the results were vastly different. Fans everywhere embraced the new "dancing Cosmo," and a video of the performance went viral within twenty-four hours. I spent the entire next week doing undercover news interviews and eavesdropping on conversations across campus. Students were going crazy trying to figure out who I was. Before I went to bed each night I read thousands of video comments speculating as to whether or not I was a girl. There were hundreds of variations of the same argument—"Guys just can't move that way."

One comment stuck out to me in particular: "This guy has to be gay."

I smiled when I read it, because it was true.

Needless to say, I got to "suit up" quite a bit more after that. From that point on, each time I donned the Cosmo mask, I made sure to do so with my full personality. I continued to make mascot dance videos throughout my time at BYU and was able to open some truly remarkable opportunities for myself—and for the university. I was invited by ESPN to perform live on the College Football Awards show, and NBC Sports even dubbed 2017–18 the "Year of the Mascot" in honor of Cosmo's viral influence. By tapping into my desire to perform on an all-girl college dance team, I gave BYU's Cosmo international recognition and influenced mascot programs all across the country. Just like in my missionary service, I found I was better able to entertain and uplift others as I connected to who I truly am. As Cosmo, I wasn't successful in spite of being gay—I was successful because of it.

I believe the Savior knows that I'm gay, understands it, and can use that to work through me for good. I am most successful, most fruitful, and most connected to the Spirit when I am genuine and true to myself. Though in the framework of mortality my eternal identity traits are sometimes labeled as feminine or masculine, gay or straight, I believe my Heavenly Parents see them simply as parts of who I am. Through the Savior, I've learned I can embrace the feminine parts of my identity without shame or apology, and be better off for it.

Jesus made flowers, so I can too.

3

TELL IT ON THE MOUNTAIN

I HOPPED OUT of the rickety safari Jeep in front of an old wooden sign emblazoned in bright yellow lettering—"Machme Gate, Elevation: 1800M."

Is this real life? I thought as I looked up at the mountain above me. Honestly, I couldn't see much—a jungle of trees and vines climbed higher and higher until it was lost in an expanse of white, billowy clouds.

Dust stirred as the old metal door of the Jeep slammed shut and I made my way around to the back to grab our supplies. Our intended "minimalist" hike up the mountain didn't feel so minimalist as I hoisted the heavy bags from the trunk onto my shoulders. We each had enough food and water to last four days, in addition to some basic outerwear and camping gear. The ration cap on our food seemed like the perfect motivation to hit my dad's extreme goal—to successfully complete the nine-day summit hike in less than half of that time, unassisted.

I was excited to be traveling again. My brother Sam, my sister Hannah, and I usually spent summers with our dad. We'd spent the previous July white-water rafting and hiking throughout the western United States, and the summer before on a trip through

Europe, exploring cities, hiking in the Alps, touring cathedrals, and, by my request, visiting art museums.

While my dad checked us into the national park, my two younger siblings helped me carry everything over to the scale station to be weighed. My backpack, filled mostly with water, trail mix, and tarps, weighed in at just under 30 kilograms. I wasn't sure whether to wince or smile as I did the conversion math in my head. This would undoubtedly prove to be the most difficult physical challenge of my life. I flashed a smile at my brother Sam as the park guide explained that he didn't think we could make it to the summit and back without any porters to help carry our supplies. Sam gave me a toothy grin, and with that we headed over to meet my dad and Hannah at the trailhead.

"Good luck!" called the park ranger as the four of us started up the mountain. "You'll need it."

During my past two years living in Utah, I had become an avid hiker. Every weekend that I wasn't performing at a football game or appearing as Cosmo at a university event, I was somewhere on a hiking trip with a group of friends. These days, Angel's Landing in Zion National Park was a breeze, and getting to the peak of Mt. Timpanogos was more of an afternoon outing than a serious trek. About twenty minutes into this hike, however, I realized that Mt. Kilimanjaro with a sixty-five-pound backpack would be no leisurely stroll through the park.

But as hard as they seemed to try, the strained, heavy straps cutting into my shoulders couldn't distract from the beauty of the landscape. Palm leaves and mossy vines hung like weighty curtains over the steep dirt path. Light came through in scattered bursts, revealing bright pops of green on the shadowy jungle floor. My eyes were drawn to the thick, braided roots that covered the ground and gave rise to heavy, twisted trunks. Beads of cool water dripped from the canopy above onto my sticky skin. As we ascended higher and higher, new plants began to appear. Bright flowers dotted the lush, green backdrop, and bushy, black-and-white colobus monkeys jumped from limb to limb, chasing each other through the dense forest.

Sam and I were moving fast, focused and in sync. After a few hours I realized we had pulled ahead and were now walking alone, together on the trail. My little brother wasn't so little anymore. I watched our feet methodically hit the ground, our long steps perfectly in line. Being around Sam was like finding twenty dollars in your pocket. He had a way of making everyone around him cooler, more carefree, and more confident. Even though I was five years older, Sam and I had been best friends ever since I could remember.

As kids we had spent countless hours in the front driveway rebounding for each other and playing one-on-one basketball. We played until our palms were semi-permanently stained black from dribbling the ball on the asphalt. I had the best three-point shot in the family until Sam came along. He played ball like it was an art, and I couldn't remember a single time I lost a pick-up game when he was on my team. We loved adventure and did almost everything together. We explored caves in stranger's fields, built handmade bed frames for our room, and made money shoveling driveways on snow days. We rode bikes around our hometown and challenged people to relay races at the city pool. We sang together, tried to cook together, and almost always stayed up late on school nights talking about the future and everything we hoped to accomplish. Now, as adults, we wore the same clothes, listened to the same music, and even had the same type of car. We were the same height, the same speed, and had the same strong, optimistic, outgoing personality.

But there was one important part of me that Sam didn't know about.

Hardly anybody did. I felt like I was constantly living a lie, and pressure to keep pretending was evident all around me. As I endlessly grappled with consequential questions of faith and sexuality, everyone around me simply assumed I was straight. Friends, family, and peers would ask me about girls and why I wasn't dating anybody. People would speculate about what kind of girl I would marry, and it seemed everyone was constantly trying to set me up on blind dates. I felt so awkward every time I lied about being too busy or too focused on school to be dating; I felt even worse when I would actually go on the dates.

But that wasn't the worst part about being "in the closet." I felt like I was completely alone. When my friends had a crush it was exciting, and people would rally to brainstorm date ideas or ways to help wingman. Meanwhile, when I had a crush, I couldn't tell anyone and was riddled with shame and guilt. I didn't have an outlet to express my fears, thoughts, or needs. I went through countless nights flattened by depression and hopelessness, and experienced extreme moments of repression and self-loathing, feeling I had no support system—no one I could to turn to. I didn't have a space to bring what I considered the darkest pieces of my soul to light.

I was altogether haunted by the fear of rejection—I had seen it happen to so many people before me. I'd watched families and friendships break apart and once-loving relationships turn distant and cold. I couldn't handle the thought of losing my friends—I couldn't fathom the pain of losing my family—but how could any of them love me if they knew I was gay? Fear led me to distance myself from the people I loved the most.

My cousin Rachel was the first to notice. Rachel and I had

always seen eye-to-eye, and she cared about me in a way I had never felt before. By miracle, we were placed in the same district in the Missionary Training Center before our Church missions. We had grown up far apart and didn't know each other well as children, but in the MTC we immediately became friends. We learned Spanish together; we learned about life together. We sent each other handwritten letters every week for two years until we were both home, then grew ever closer as we talked about our lives, shared our favorite books, and went on cross-country road trips.

Rachel saw the hopelessness I was trying to hide. On a calm November night at 1:38 a.m. in a parking lot overlooking BYU's campus, she asked me what was wrong. In that moment, I realized the pain of holding on to my secret was worse than the potential rejection that came with sharing it. I decided to trust Rachel and tell her what I was going through. Coming out to her was, and forever will be, one of the bravest things I have ever done.

It wasn't easy. It wasn't easy at all. For at least twenty minutes I was frozen. I began to hyperventilate. I was usually so in control of my body and emotions, but all of my faculties shut down. I felt uneasy, like I was going to either pass out or throw up. Rachel sat peacefully in the driver's seat and patiently waited for me to uncover the part of me I had crippled and buried for so long.

I came out in a series of sobs. I told her I was attracted to men and was suffocating from uncertainty and isolation. I expressed to her the pain I felt not knowing where I belonged and feeling like there was nobody like me. I wept. I told her I didn't know how I could live any longer feeling that way. I begged her to somehow accept me.

Rachel stayed calm as I exposed the most shame-filled, distressing pieces of my soul. She listened intently and waited until I was finished and had regained some of my composure. Then, she said four simple words that, to me, felt like the first true breath of air that I had taken in years:

"Charlie, I love you."

She stayed and talked with me for hours. She told me my sexual orientation didn't define me. I had never considered that before. She reiterated her love. She asked me questions about my experiences, and immediately believed them without pushback or doubt. She assured me that she would support me in any decision I made, and that I could always count on her if I needed a place to sort out my thoughts, feelings, or beliefs.

My heart healed a little bit that night. Coming out to Rachel was my first step in learning to trust in another person's true, unconditional love. She was willing to share the burden I had carried alone for so long. She took my shame and loved me so hard that I finally began to let some of it go.

Rachel's positive reinforcement helped me become more sure of myself, and I soon found the confidence to tell my older sisters. When I told my sister Anne, she said, "I will be whatever you want me to be." She met me with love, acceptance, and understanding. She reassured me I could trust my oldest sister, Janine, and that they both would have my back no matter what. I listened to Anne and came out to Janine a few weeks later. She cried, not because I was gay, but because she loved me so much. I saw how she cared about me, and was greatly comforted as I began to understand that no matter who I was or how I felt, her love was unconditional. Where I saw a broken, tangled, unlovable man, she saw a strong, capable, worthy soul.

Rachel, Anne, and Janine offered me trust, acceptance, and support. They gave me a space where I no longer felt I had to lie or pretend to be someone I wasn't. I knew, no matter what, I had at least three people who knew the real me—and loved me all the same.

My screaming muscles pulled me away from my thoughts and back to reality. I was in a jungle in northern Tanzania, walking next to my little brother, Sam.

Together we worked through the heat of the early afternoon, breathing heavily and leaving footprints in the dirt as we made our way up the winding trail. Our competitive natures caused us to push ourselves, but we drew encouragement and strength from each other.

I wish I could tell Sam, I thought. *I wish he could see the real me.*

I couldn't, though. If I told him, and he rejected me, there would be no way to go back. Our relationship could be permanently wrecked. There would be no way to backpedal if it didn't go well. Sam was one of the most important people in my entire life. I couldn't risk losing him or changing the way he viewed me. Even thinking about coming out to him stressed me out. I decided to push the thought out of my head and began to focus instead on the foliage around me. Everything in nature seemed to work so perfectly.

Everything except for me . . .

I felt sick.

"What are you thinking about?" Sam ventured. He knew me well—I usually wasn't so quiet for so long. As soon as he said the words, my gut dropped and apprehension shot through my veins.

"Uh . . . the . . . just the trees," I panicked.

Sam was eighteen years old and had just graduated from high school. He was planning to come to BYU with me in the fall and wanted to serve a mission for the Church, just as I had. I had always been a role model for him. I knew he looked up to me, intellectually, emotionally, and especially spiritually. Would he still view me as a role model if he knew I was gay? I was trying so hard to stay close to God, but how could I help Sam figure out anything about life or faith when I myself felt so ridiculously confused?

Even though I had experienced some really beautiful, affirming moments coming out to Rachel and my sisters, I still didn't think I could tell Sam. At least, not now. He seemed too young. He might be too immature to handle it. Scarier still, Sam was type-A heterosexual. He was a ladies' man, like a high school jock ripped straight out of a Disney movie. Coming out to him seemed so, so much more difficult. A girl could understand being attracted to men. Rachel and my sisters weren't disgusted by the idea. But Sam? Would he be as understanding, or would he be repulsed?

Then, as I looked over at my brother with his absurdly large backpack, tent poles dangling off the back, I got the "coming-out feeling."*

I had to tell him. I had to tell him here. I had to tell him now.

My breath became increasingly shallow. Again, I began to hyperventilate.

"Are you okay, bro?" Sam asked. "For being the 'world's most athletic mascot,' you sure aren't in very good shape!" He loved to tease me about the way ESPN had described Cosmo during the last football season.

* The coming-out feeling is the way you might feel if you had to speak, unprepared, in front of a group of 100,000 people. It is the feeling of the Spirit telling you to stand up and bear your testimony on Sunday, except magnified by at least 7,000. It's a mixture of queasiness, exasperation, and hope, so potent and so powerful that you aren't sure your legs will be able to support you if it stays in your heart (and stomach) much longer.

As hard as I tried, I couldn't manage to reply. I continued gasping for air, struggling to reclaim control of my hysterical lungs.

Sam's smirk turned into a genuine look of concern. "Come on, there's a fallen tree over there, we can go sit on it and take a break. I'm pretty tired, too," he said, trying to mask the worry in his voice.

"It's not . . . the mountain . . ." I managed to gasp between breaths. I slowed my pace. My soul felt heavier than the weight on my back.

"What is it, then?" he replied.

"Sam."

I paused.

"I'm . . . gay."

"What?"

"I'm . . . I'm not attracted to girls. I'm . . . I'm gay, Sam. I'm attracted to guys," I replied hesitantly.

We walked a few steps in silence.

"Are you sure?" he questioned.

"Yeah," I said matter-of-factly. I looked over at his face. His mind seemed to be on overdrive, trying to process what I had said.

"It's not a choice?" he asked, his voice sounding thick.

"Why would I choose this?" I asked earnestly.

His body language told me that the somber realization of my predicament was sinking in—the complications that being gay might pose to my relationships, my worship, and other social and cultural aspects of my life.

"What are you going to do?" he asked expectantly.

"I don't know," I said, unsure how the conversation was going.

We walked in silence for a few steps.

"Bro, well, I love you and I don't care," he started without hesitation. "I mean, I trust you. I know whatever you choose will be the right thing, and I will support you no matter what. I love you, Charlie. We're brothers. We're tight," Sam said.

I looked over at him as the apprehension withdrew from my body, not sure what to say.

He looked back at me, straight in the eyes. "This doesn't change anything. This doesn't change anything at all," he replied.

Nothing did change. We took a water break on a mossy log and shared a Snickers bar as he started asking me follow-up questions. He apologized for things he had said or done in the past that might have made it harder for me to trust him. He asked me what I needed from him and assured me he would do anything he could to support me. We promised each other that, moving forward, we would be more open and honest about what we were going through. By the time my dad and Hannah caught up to us, Sam and I were as normal as ever, jumping off rocks and joking about how we were so much faster than our old man.

I hiked the rest of the mountain with a vitality I hadn't felt before. Sam had helped me summit my personal mountain, and as a result, I felt invigorated emotionally and physically. The four of us moved as a team, without bothering to pause at rest stops or designated campsites. The following days felt surreal, like a mini sub-life within my existence. With increases in elevation came frequent changes in terrain and wildlife; I marveled as we climbed over jagged cliffs and walked through endless fields of broken obsidian. When we surfaced over the first thick layer of clouds we yelled at the top of our lungs, our voices echoing out into the world below.

Now that Sam knew I was gay, my cheerful heart constantly filled me with new energy. Hannah and I chased each other down valley paths, and I entertained tired hikers by doing backflips on ledges that seemed to look over the entire world. After a long second day of walking beneath the sweltering sun, we dipped ourselves in a frigid mountain stream and set up camp. The four of us took turns telling stories around our small propane tank as our food rations cooked, until chilling shadows crept down from the mountain and enveloped the entire campsite.

At night Sam and I lay close in our narrow tent and complained about the rocky ground that cut into our ribs. He said he would give anything to have a can of Dr. Pepper, and I said the same about Pringles. We spent hours awake, talking about all the things we had never felt able to share with each other. Sam asked me dozens of questions about my life, my faith, my doubts, and my orientation, and I answered all of them without fear or hesitation. I explained to him how I felt there was something more to being gay than just sexual orientation—something that was connected to who I am on a much deeper level. He knew me, so he understood, though neither of us had words to articulate exactly what it was. I told him how much closer I felt to God now that I was seeking heavenly guidance without shame or reservation. I conveyed that staying close to the Lord was my greatest desire, and I thanked Sam for expressing trust in me.

"Of course I trust you, Charlie," he said. "I know you. I know your heart. You never have to worry about what I think. I'm with you 'til the end."

His words helped me trust myself a little more as well.

I felt closer to Sam than ever before.

When cold and uncomfortable ground still precluded sleep, we crawled out of our tent to watch the stars rotate above us. They flickered like diamonds in the moonless sky and illuminated our cold breath. I almost felt like I could reach up and grab them.

Later, when the deep blue of night faded into the soft light of dawn, we laced up our shoes, packed up our gear, and kept moving on toward base camp.

We arrived to base camp dirty and cold, just three days after starting our trek (though it felt more like three years). Large, oblong rocks positioned themselves all around us, causing the wind to howl as it whistled between them. I didn't feel like I was on Earth. There was a complete lack of vegetation, and our only companions were a few large ravens squawking and circling ahead, scavenging for food left from hikers before. We rationed what was left of our trail mix, drank as much as we could, and passed out on the rocks as the wind beat against our feeble tents. Just after 2:00 a.m. we roused our tired bones and began the last stretch up a steep, rocky path to the summit of the mountain. Harsh winds at negative temperatures ripped through our thin outerwear and tempted us to lie down and rest—but we had come this far, and we wouldn't risk missing daybreak at 19,341 feet above sea level.

A few hours later, Sam, Hannah, my dad, and I stood on top of the tallest freestanding mountain on Earth and waited for the sunrise. Light moved slowly across the sparse, volcanic terrain and scattered pastel hues on the glaciers surrounding the summit. Time stood still as the sun broke through the curved horizon and cast a brilliant, all-encompassing glow on the world around us. As the new light illuminated the cold, dark landscape, it seemed to echo the way I felt inside—brighter, and more beautiful.

After the sunrise I took off my gloves to snap a few photos, but my hands immediately began to freeze. I tried to ignore the cold that pierced through my jacket and bask in the immaculate view before me.

"This is easily the most beautiful thing I've ever seen," I said through shivers.

"It's amazing," Hannah agreed, shaking violently.

The four of us stood side by side, drinking in the panoramic view for as long as we could.

"So . . . how long are we going to pretend we don't all want to get back down?" Sam joked after a few moments.

"He said it, not me!" I laughed.

"Let's get out of here before we freeze to death," Dad agreed.

We took one last look at the vista, then started back down the mountain. Graced by the new light of morning, we skated down slopes of loose rock until we made it back to base camp. Once there, we packed up our tents and assessed our dwindling water supply.

"Not much. Everything we do have tastes horrible," Dad reported. "Should we just hit it hard and try to make it all the way down today?" he suggested.

"Let's do it," Hannah concurred.

Sam and I gave each other a look halfway between a grimace and a grin, and with that we set off to finish the hike.

For the rest of the day we pounded down the opposite side of the mountain. I forced my eyes to fight the sleepiness that was accumulating, and my sore muscles ached under the remaining weight in my backpack. I knew we were nearing the end of the trail when the landscape returned to a misty jungle. With every switchback, I ached to see the parking lot that marked the finish line. For the sake of my knees, I prayed it would come soon.

Just when I thought I couldn't take a single step farther, we rounded a corner and the end of the trail came into view. Since our 2:00 a.m. wake-up call at base camp, we had hiked for over sixteen hours without stopping. We slumped on the ground by a trail marker and gulped fresh water until we saw the same rusty, old Jeep break over the horizon.

A few minutes later, as I packed our travel-worn bags back into the vehicle, I thought about my journey over the past few days. It had pushed my physical limits and made me dig into stores of energy I didn't know I had. The trails were beautiful, rife with plants and animals I had only ever dreamed of seeing firsthand. Watching the sunrise at the summit had been nothing short of magical.

But as extraordinary as it all was, the most incredible part of the journey had been coming out to Sam. I made my way around to the side of the Jeep to hop in next to him. I sat down and slammed the door shut with a tired, grateful smile. There was nothing that could come between me and my brother. We were together, through thick and thin.

4

LIVING IN THE LIGHT

THERE'S NOTHING QUITE like the rolling hills of a Missouri hay field. The green terrain, dotted with golden round bales, extends as far as the eye can see. Hay brings with it the fresh, grassy smell of summer, and the whole world feels clean and new. Stacking hay was my favorite chore growing up. My dad had a bright orange Kubota tractor that we used to move bales to the edge of the field. The shuttle clutch made it a pretty easy tractor to learn on, but I still felt like farm royalty whenever I got to drive it. I stacked bale after bale, slowly clearing the field and creating endless rows of hay that my older sisters and I could play on all year long.

The first time I was trusted to stack bales without supervision was a big moment for me. I spent the whole afternoon by myself, driving back and forth across the field and controlling the hydraulic arms of the tractor. Like clockwork, I stacked the last bale right as dusk set in. I proudly turned the tractor around and set out to park it in its usual spot.

After a few moments I realized something wasn't right. The tractor was having a hard time moving forward. I pushed on the throttle and the engine roared. It started to make a horrible grinding noise as it shook along. Black smoke billowed out of the exhaust pipe and the Kubota moved forward in awkward lurches, struggling to maintain momentum.

All of a sudden the screaming engine went quiet and the tractor stopped moving. I jumped off nervously to see if I could figure out what had gone wrong. To my dismay, I realized that rather than lifting the arms as I drove across the field, I had kept them down, and the bale spike had buried into the ground. When I looked behind me, I saw a long, deep trench cutting across the freshly mowed field. Dirt was upheaved in a jagged line that began all the way at the base of the hay bales, some hundred meters away. I felt my stomach drop immediately.

Dad is going to kill me, I thought.

I quickly climbed back onto the tractor to see if I could start it up and back the spike out of the ground, but to no avail. The tractor was broken, and there was nothing I could do. I hopped off, then ran as fast as I could across the field to the front gate. *Maybe if I can get there before he comes to get me, Dad won't see the tractor and I can buy myself some time*, I thought wishfully. As I ran, I imagined him yelling at me, telling me I was a terrible farmhand, and never letting me stack bales ever again.

He pulled up right as I reached the gate.

"Did you park the Kubota?" he asked as I hopped in his white, flatbed Ford.

"Yeah," I squeaked. Little did he know how "parked" the Kubota actually was.

"Awesome. Good job!"

I shut the truck door with a queasy stomach. I knew he would eventually find out what had happened, but even still, keeping it a secret didn't feel good. I was so embarrassed. After about thirty seconds of intolerable silence I couldn't take it any longer and decided to bring my secret to light.

"Hey . . . Dad . . ." I said nervously.

"What's up?" he asked.

"I . . . I didn't park the tractor. Actually, I broke it."

I explained what had happened and apologized for my carelessness. The steam of uneasiness that had been building inside me began to let out as I came clean and directed him to where the tractor was. When we neared the crime scene, I braced myself for his reaction.

"Well, that's a pretty big trench you dug there," he said.

"It's awful, isn't it?" I replied with regret.

"Terrible," he said with a laugh. "Let's go home and eat. We can take care of this mess tomorrow."

Maya Angelou once wrote, "There is no greater agony than bearing an untold story inside you." Her words ring true to me. The feeling I'd had before I told my dad about the tractor was dreadful. I was stuck in my own head. Paranoia and embarrassment impaired rational thinking and I vilified my dad. I expected him to be angry and unforgiving, when in reality he was kind and lighthearted.

The anxiety and fear I'd felt over the tractor mirror my years before coming out as gay. Before I brought my identity to light, I was riddled with agony and despair. I felt I could never break through the surface. Thankfully, I have also learned the inverse of Ms. Angelou's words to be true: there is no greater *joy* than *releasing* the untold story inside you. By coming out and sharing my true self, I have found joy sweeter than I had ever imagined.

One of my favorite children's hymns is called "Teach Me to

Walk in the Light." I used to sit on the front row of my Primary class and belt the song at the top of my lungs. Coming out has led me to think a lot about the contrast of walking in the dark versus the light. When I covered myself in darkness, I was more susceptible to the effects of self-deprecation and shame. When I took courageous leaps of faith and began to walk in the light, I gained confidence and hope.

I've seen that the adversary works best in darkness. Feelings of worthlessness, doubt, and confusion are amplified when they are tucked away and hidden. Covering and holding on to hurt and shame can lead to paranoia, sleepless nights, and increased feelings of isolation and self-doubt. Without any outlet, my life became a downward spiral that felt entirely suffocating. When I hid my story, I blinded myself to my worth as a divine child of God and pulled away from others. Darkness manipulated the voices in my head and beguiled me into believing I was worthless, hopeless, and alone. Darkness entertains the lie that we have no value and that our lives are neither important nor worthwhile.

For me, the most damaging result of holding onto my story was shame. Like a bacteria, shame thrives in darkness. The word *shame* itself conveys a sense of humiliation, worthlessness, and a desire to hide and withdraw. When we allow shame to take hold of our hearts, we isolate ourselves, cutting off light and love. Shame lies to us, saying we are unlovable and alone.

Galatians 5:22 tells us that "the fruit of the Spirit is love, joy, peace, longsuffering, gentleness, goodness, faith." The fruit of shame is self-hate, depression, anxiety, impatience, paranoia, nervousness, and delusion. Shame does not, and never has, come from God. From the very beginning, the adversary has used shame to trick us into hiding from God's light. Satan's first tactic after Adam and Eve partook of the forbidden fruit was to riddle them with shame. At their most vulnerable state, Lucifer mocked them for being naked and urged them to run away and hide. Adam and Eve then hurriedly "hid themselves from the presence of the Lord God amongst the trees of the garden" (Genesis 3:8).

When I let internalized shame gain control of my life, I felt unworthy of my relationship with my family and of my divine rights as a child of God. I doubled down in humiliation and filled my own mind with lies about my worth. Rather than seeking to connect, I hid from the presence of God. I was deceived into believing I deserved the shame and self-deprecation I subjected myself to.

I used to lie awake at night and think about Judgment Day. I imagined myself standing in a white, cloudy arena surrounded by the generations of my entire extended family. God sat in an intricate golden throne in front of me, and all were watching as my life was projected onto a massive screen. There was an audible gasp from the crowd when the screen displayed the world from my vantage point and revealed that I was attracted to men. My mom wept on the sidelines, repeatedly asking herself, "Why?" My sisters called out, "How could you do this to us?" and my dad and brother looked down at me in disgust. God hammered a wooden gavel and the floor opened up beneath me, revealing a fiery pit. I looked at my family as I fell down into the pit, yelling "I'm sorry" over and over again.

What actually happened when my family found out I am gay was far from the theatrical scenario I used to imagine. My mom expressed perfect love and a sincere desire for me to be happy. My sisters all told me they loved me for who I am and would do anything they could to support me. My brother told me he trusted me to make my own decisions and would stand by me no matter what, and my dad hugged me and told me he was proud of the fearless man I had become.

Sister Sharon Eubank taught, "One of the fundamental needs we have in order to grow is to stay connected to the source of light—Jesus Christ. He is the source of our power, the Light and Life of the World. Without a strong connection to Him, we begin to spiritually die. Knowing that, Satan tries to exploit the world pressures we all face. He works to dim our light, short-circuit the connection, cut off the power supply, leaving us alone in the dark. These pressures are common conditions in mortality, but Satan works hard to isolate us and tell us we are the only one experiencing them" (*Ensign*, May 2019).

The adversary used shame to short-circuit my connection with God. Shame was the reason it took me years to ask real, honest questions about my identity. I thought Heavenly Father was indignant, imposing, and embarrassed of me. I felt I had to hide, when, in reality, I had loving, compassionate Heavenly Parents who wanted me to draw near to Them. When I finally opened up to God, I realized He wasn't waiting in heaven swinging a gavel, eager to send me to hell. Instead, I felt assured that He is the architect of my soul, a merciful, all-knowing being who sent His Only Begotten Son to save me. God wants us to have hope and salvation, not despondency and torment. Being open with the Lord through sincere prayer has helped me feel His divine love.

I've noticed a troubling pattern among LGBTQ individuals often sparked by internalized shame and intensified by a lack of visible love and acceptance. I know of many wonderful, talented people who turn to unhealthy coping mechanisms because they don't have a way to operate in the light. Whether intentionally or not, in family and social circles their identities seem taboo, and they become plagued by isolation and guilt. With no positive outlets to bring their stories to light, some begin to operate in dark, anonymous spaces.

The most common outlet is pornography. This is an easy way to explore sexuality without anybody knowing, but pornography use is harmful and leads to unhealthy views on relationships. Additionally, the shame centered around pornography is often toxic and leads to a sense of emptiness. When amplified by existing shame from same-sex attraction, pornography becomes emotionally and spiritually destructive.

Another dangerous trend is the use of internet chat sites and anonymous dating apps as an outlet. On difficult, sleepless nights, many have sought anonymous sources for approval and affirmation, instead of turning to the people who truly care for them. When they feel depressed and misunderstood, they go to places where they know their sexuality won't be an issue. Imagine completely hating yourself, then finding someone who likes the parts of you that you despise. Many have found themselves overwhelmed and taken advantage of after innocently trusting a stranger. Certainly not everyone that uses a chat site or a dating app has malicious intentions, but I know many good, good people who have naively put their trust in the wrong person. Lack of confidence and self-worth has led them down a path of emotionally damaging decisions. Innocent, beautiful souls have been catfished and abused because they never had the chance to develop healthy attitudes and boundaries in the light.

The risk of not providing a healthy, safe environment where LGBTQ individuals can voice their concerns can be as serious as porn addiction and sexual abuse. In some cases, it can be as serious as suicidal ideation.

I show visible love and support to the LGBTQ community because at baptism I made a covenant with God to "bear one another's burdens, that they may be light" (Mosiah 18:8). I promised God to lift the burden of shame that others feel and provide a space where they can walk in the light. I invite all to prayerfully do the same. We never know who might be hiding behind a mask. If you have family members or friends who are "in the closet," chances are they are watching you closely. They probably know everything you have ever said about gay people. We must no longer carelessly allow our words and actions to drive innocent souls into darkness.

My sister Anne understood this. What I now jokingly refer to as the "Anne Approach" was her way of showing me visible love and support before she received verbal confirmation that I was gay. Anne is remarkably emotionally intuitive, and she began to suspect I was having a hard time after I returned home from my mission. She payed close attention to how I talked about girls I was trying to date and how I interacted with others. When she considered that I might be gay, instead of confronting me about it, she began to study. She read articles, blogs, and journals about gay members of our church and educated herself on how to best support them.

One night Anne texted me and my brother Sam in a group chat. I can still see her text in my mind. She wrote three paragraphs explaining how if either of us were gay, she wouldn't care, and would love us all the same. She emphasized that, no matter what we did, she would love us and always be there. She began to do things like this often. She dropped hints that she was trustworthy and willing to listen. She didn't assume I was gay, but gave every sign to say that if I was, I would be safe with her. I knew whenever I was ready to come out, I could trust her. I had faith that whenever I felt low and lonely, I could talk to her instead of a stranger.

As oppressive as darkness can be, I've also seen that God works best in the light. In the New Testament, John taught, "God is light, and in him is no darkness at all" (1 John 1:5).Living in the light allows us to access Christ's enabling power and feel His transcendent love.

When I reached out and was vulnerable with others, I allowed myself to breathe. I filled my void of loneliness with connection and community, and I found humanity and validation that brought peace to my tired soul. I caught remarkable glimpses of humankind's extraordinary ability to love unconditionally, despite my challenges or perceived flaws. By giving voice to my deepest secrets and fears, I found I was greeted by a support system I didn't know I had. I felt optimism when I saw that others were willing to listen and help carry my pain. I was reminded of my divine potential and the unparalleled worth of each human life.

Jesus Christ said, "Behold I am the light; I have set an example for you" (3 Nephi 18:16). The example that Christ set was one of love and inclusion. He often sat and surrounded Himself with people who were deemed unclean, worthless, or sinful by society. He saw all as equal children of God and shattered the idea that anyone should be marginalized or separated into camps. By following His example and seeking to see the worth in others, we elevate our ability to love and serve those around us. As we do so, we take upon ourselves His sacred charge to be the "light of the world." Christ's perfect example taught that showing love and support is not a compromise of moral values—it's how we allow others to live in the light.

By being vulnerable and accessing the Savior's all-encompassing power, I crawled out of the layers of darkness and shame I had been covered in. I forgave myself for the years I had spent hiding and running away. I became mindful of self-deprecating thoughts and matured in my ability to identify whether guilt was meaning-driven or if it was just shame masking itself as godly sorrow, driven only by culture or fear. Though heavy and overwhelming, through the Savior, darkness and shame can be overcome. Jesus Christ beat my shame when He bled in the garden and hung on the cross. He truly did "bear the shame of the world" (Jacob 1:8).

Many of my fondest college memories include practicing with the BYU Dunk Team. Each practice was front-loaded with push-ups, pull-ups, sit-ups, and stair circuits. After putting in a good workout, we would head back to the gymnastics room and train each other in tumbling, parkour, and trampoline. During football season we planned death-defying stunts that entertained hundreds of thousands of people, and throughout basketball season we performed acrobatic trampoline dunk shows. We soared through the air, flipping our bodies and passing basketballs in perfect rhythm.

In the fall of 2015 I secured a spot on the BYU Dunk Team. I came in bright and optimistic with three other new guys, but I quickly realized the team wasn't what I had expected. Many of the returning teammates had known each other for years and were close friends. All of them had superhuman skills or talents, and I felt insecure as I compared myself to them. They were strong, talented, and professionally trained. I felt out of place and stupid for thinking I could hang with them without any previous training.

With a jumbled mix of new talent, the team dynamic felt uncomfortable and off. The awkward division on the team made already strenuous practices almost unbearable for me. Stunts fell and ideas clashed in the cliquey, competitive environment that prevailed.

One afternoon, following our usual warm-up, our coach shared a spiritual message instead of leading us out to the track to run sprints. He talked about the blessings he had seen from adversity in his life, then asked if anyone had any thoughts they would like to share. We sat in silence for a while, each of us staring down at the gymnastics floor and waiting for somebody else to speak.

One by one, teammates opened up about challenges they had faced and what they had learned from them. I had no idea that these guys, who seemed strong, capable, and perfect, had been through such heartbreaking trials and adversity. I was amazed at their resilience and how they had used their challenges to grow and come closer to the Savior. The Spirit in the room was overpowering.

I felt prompted to speak up and talk about the challenges I had faced during my parents' divorce. I got emotional when I recounted how my siblings and I had come together and grown stronger when we were forced to adapt to a new family dynamic. My teammates listened intently and validated my story. I learned I was not the only one who had divorced parents. We spent the entire practice sitting in a circle on the floor and sharing sacred, important moments that shaped who we are. After two hours passed, we finished with a prayer, then played around on the spring floor until night fell.

From that point on, our mishmash group of break dancers, tumblers, and trickers became a team. We carpooled to parties and rearranged our class schedules so we could eat together every day. Once-dreaded practices became my favorite part of my college experience. We trusted each other with our very lives, and we were able to pull off stunts and shows that previously had only been dreamed of. We became roommates, friends, and groomsmen at each other's weddings. The camaraderie that stemmed from that one practice made a significant impact on me and gave me lifelong brothers. By being vulnerable with one another and sharing our stories, we became unified as one.

Openness and vulnerability build connection. Sometimes sharing our truth comes with a high risk, but for me, the rewards of taking that risk have been unparalleled. Just as divulging deeply personal stories on the Dunk Team led to unity and understanding, sharing who I am with friends and family has strengthened my relationships and led me to increased happiness. Hiding kept me in darkness; coming out led me to light.

My life is far sweeter when I step out from the shadows. While I once hid away in layers of darkness, I now happily choose to live in the light.

5

FLIPPING OUT

I WALKED INTO my mom's living room to find I was the first one awake. A small tree glittered in the corner, flanked by a charming border of carefully wrapped gifts. I quietly padded across the floor and slid my body underneath the tree, feeling for one of the softer presents to use as a pillow.

While I lay there, I remembered the first time I woke up early on Christmas day, years ago. Unbeknownst to me, my sister Anne had walked into the living room just minutes before. I about had a heart attack when she jumped out to scare me. When we were finally done laughing, we positioned ourselves under the tree and looked up at the layered levels of sparkling evergreen. It was magical. We lay there for almost an hour, breathing in the sharp pine and talking about the birth of the Savior until the rest of the family woke up and the Christmas festivities could begin.

Now, as I watched the lights cast a golden glow on the dark pine needles, I thought about how this Christmas had a childlike charm I hadn't felt since then. The previous two holidays I had been a missionary. They were incredible, but not really comparable to the rest. Before that, Christmas break had been weird. It was difficult learning how to balance time between my parents after their divorce.

The last Christmas I had spent at home, however, had been my worst. I had just received my mission call, and while my whole family was thrilled, I felt terrified. All I could think about was how disappointed they might be if my same-sex attraction somehow forced me to come home early. The dread ate away at me all through the holiday, pushing me deeper and deeper into distress as I imagined horrifying mission scenarios.

Thankfully, my fears were just that—fears. My mission was beautiful, and I felt hope for the future. These days, I didn't worry about same-sex attraction. I felt like serving an honorable mission had sealed off those feelings. Even the scarring memories that my struggle had left me with were buried so deep that they felt distant and inconsequential. I felt like the war was over.

I had been dating all semester at BYU and, even though all my friends said I was too picky, I felt pretty successful. I went on a lot of first dates, and I was hopeful I could eventually find a girl I wanted to date seriously. I finally felt on track for the life I had planned.

My thoughts were interrupted when Hannah walked into the room.

"Hey! You're up early," she said.

"I can't help it—I get too excited," I replied.

"Janine and Anne will probably get here soon . . . think I'll be able to wake up Sam?" she asked with a laugh.

An hour later we all sat around the Christmas tree, accompanied by the crunch of wrapping paper as we took turns opening presents. My brothers-in-law made jokes about our strict "youngest to oldest" order, and my new niece and nephews ripped open their gifts with excited giggles. Having them there made everything seem so lively and full.

The little kids seemed to like the packaging more than the actual gifts. We passed the day playing with boxes and paper before moving on to their new toys. When four o'clock rolled around we all took to the kitchen and helped prepare for the Christmas feast. My mom's roast beef stole the show, paired with deviled eggs, green beans, and mashed potatoes. Each of us piled our plates high and scooted chairs around the small kitchen table. For dessert, my brother and I had a competition to see who could eat the most chocolate sheet cake. We spent the evening as a family singing hymns around the piano, playing dominos, and talking about our favorite Christmas memories.

At night, after everyone had either left or gone to bed, I went out to the front yard and stretched my wrists in preparation for one of my favorite Christmas activities. Many years prior, on Christmas night, I had gone outside to walk around my neighborhood and look at the lights. I watched them dance in the wind against the brick houses and reflect off of the low, powdered clouds. I was so happy that the only way I could think to express how I felt was by doing a backflip. In the years that followed, tumbling by the glow of Christmas lights had become my own unconventional tradition.

In the faint, multicolored glimmer of the lights, I began flipping through the crisp winter air. I spent at least forty-five minutes on the cold, crunchy grass doing series of handsprings, tucks, aerials, and layouts. If it weren't for the cold, I could have spent the entire night there in the yard.

Just before I turned into a block of ice, I went back inside to warm up on the couch that was making a weeklong cameo as my makeshift bed. I went through my usual nightly routine—read a few scripture verses on my phone, knelt to pray, and set an alarm for the morning. When sleep failed to come, I began scrolling through social media, watching mostly dance, cheer, and parkour videos, as usual.

As I scrolled, I came across a picture of a guy that made me pause. He looked cool. I clicked on his profile and started browsing through his pictures.

I wonder what he's like, I thought as I continued scrolling through his page.

I felt the nervous, light sensation of butterflies tighten in my stomach.

For the past ten years I had attributed every thought, feeling, or attraction I had to *anything* other than being gay. Whenever I felt drawn to a guy, I convinced myself it was because he was talented, athletic, or popular. I told myself that I simply wanted to be like him and fit in with his friends. By the same token, whenever I was around a girl who was talented, athletic, or popular, I forced my brain to read admiration as a crush. I was a master at lying to myself—it was almost second nature.

I kept scrolling. I didn't want to leave his page.

When I realized what was happening, I immediately tried to camouflage it with the creative lies I had always told myself. But for some reason, this time, it didn't work. My brain couldn't break away from reality. There were no feasible lies, no mental gymnastics that could mask what I was feeling. It was clear: I didn't want to be *like* him, I wanted to be *with* him.

"This can't be happening," I said under my breath.

In dramatic fashion, I threw my phone. It clattered as it landed on the hardwood floor. I started shaking, unable to breathe or focus, as shame crept up from the buried depths of my mind.

You're disgusting. You're a freak, I told myself.

Sick uneasiness bled through me. My mind was inundated with questions and fears: *Wasn't I healed of same-sex attraction? I had fervently prayed it would go away. I'd been completely faithful and served a worthy, full-time mission. Wasn't I supposed to be fixed?* My thoughts were frantic. I didn't understand how I could still be attracted to men when I was living the gospel as fully as I possibly could. Was my virtue not enough?

The darkness swallowed me whole. Every future I had imagined for myself vanished. The entire framework of my life crumbled, and I felt buried beneath the rubble. Sleepless hours passed as I lay paralyzed by the loss of my future, staring into nothing. The magic of Christmas was long gone.

When the light of early morning strained through the glass panels on the front door, I mindlessly threw on my tennis shoes, stepped outside, and ran.

I didn't want to think. I didn't want to be.

I didn't know what to do, so I just ran until I couldn't run anymore.

6

GLASS CASTLE

WHAT DO YOU do when the future you envisioned completely dissolves?

My mom grew up in a small town in Alberta, Canada, where the corn grows high and the earth lies flat. Her five older siblings quickly dubbed her the "golden child" because she was as close to perfect as just about anybody can get. My uncles still joke with me about how she opened her daily journal entries with lines from her favorite hymns. My mom really was incredible—she was top of her high school class, played the piano like Mozart, and was crowned "Sweetheart Queen" during homecoming.

After high school, Mom moved to the States and began studying nursing at Brigham Young University. She spent her free time volunteering at local hospitals, running service organizations, and dancing with my aunt at the Star Palace (they say that was the place to be back then). At twenty-two she met my dad, a handsome, charismatic football player, and they got married and sealed the following year in the Cardston Alberta Temple.

My parents moved to Missouri, where Mom worked at the local hospital while Dad finished his degree and worked cattle day in and day out. After they had Janine, Anne, and me, they moved into a big, red, brick farmhouse. Mom quit her job at the hospital to focus on what she saw as a more difficult, more important career—raising children. She took us to the library every week and read to us every night. She went to parent-teacher conferences, volunteered to chaperone on field trips, and drove her old Buick through muddy fields at 5:00 a.m. so we could bottle-feed our calves before school.

Even after having Sam and Hannah, my mom never missed my sporting events or extracurricular activities. Every Friday morning there was a check for lunch money in my backpack. When I would forget the backpack (as I often did), it was almost always already at the school before the bus even dropped me off. To many, my mom was an angel; she served and supported our community with extraordinary intelligence, talent, and devotion.

On Sunday mornings, I woke up to the smell and sound of beef chuck roast searing on the stovetop. My dad often had Church leadership meetings or loose cattle to deal with, so Mom was left to find lost shoes, tie neckties, and usher me and my siblings out the door as she threw the meat in the crockpot and slipped into her sling-back pumps. On weeknights she took me from rec league basketball games to Boy Scouts, all the while running errands and juggling my older sisters' parties, soccer practices, and school events. The "golden child" grew up to be the golden mom.

In the years that followed, my dad's cattle operation became incredibly successful, and he began contracting land for residential development. He converted hundreds of acres of farmland into upscale, suburban neighborhoods. At that time, I wanted nothing more than to be an architect, and my dad let me design many of the homes he built. My older sisters would do construction cleanup, and I would tour prospective buyers around model homes, spouting off specs about the materials used and square footage of each bedroom. Everything about my family seemed perfect, but unfortunately the perfection wouldn't last forever.

2008 was a hard year for the Birds. My dad began to travel a lot, leaving the rest of us, especially my mom, with increased responsibilities at home. He experienced a shift in his faith and decided that he no longer believed nor wanted to participate in our church. As my parents were trying to work through my dad's frequent absences and dramatic shift in views, the U.S. housing market crash and the subsequent financial recession hit hard. Our family went completely bankrupt and lost all land, cattle, homes, and physical assets. My parents ended up tangled in a complicated separation. My dad moved out shortly after, and subsequently filed for divorce.

While my mom had once been the poised matriarch of a model family, she now suddenly found herself surrounded by gossip, hearsay, and scandal. Her life had been a glass castle, but the foundation crumbled and it all came shattering down around her. At forty-three years old, she was forced to start her life completely over, without a home, husband, or job.

I was fifteen at the time, and I spent the next few years watching my mom piece her life back together. As I watched her work through her unexpected future, I learned three lessons that would eventually save me when I, too, had to face an unexpected future.

1. TAKE THINGS ONE DAY AT A TIME.

After the divorce, I was acutely aware that my mom particularly struggled when looking at life in big-picture terms. Many nights she had panic attacks as she thought about the uncertainty of her future. There was no road map and no guarantee that anything she did would help her heal or bring happiness. There was no "right" way to be a broke, single, divorced mother. When she thought about the future as a whole, she became fearful, anxious, and depressed; she became overwhelmed by doubt and insecurity.

As the weeks went by, I noticed my mom did much better when she put more focus on what her life should look like *tomorrow* rather than what it might look like in ten years. She found a place to live and applied for a job at the healthcare facility closest to our hometown. She worked hard, and put in long, twelve-hour nursing shifts at night. During the day she often filled in as a substitute teacher for the local school district. She got by as she focused on small things every day to look forward to, whether basketball games or Church activities. She stayed true to who she was and took things one day at a time, trusting the Lord to move her in the right direction.

During His ministry, Jesus instructed His followers to trust that God would clothe them day by day. In the Sermon on the Mount, He said, "Why take ye thought for raiment? Consider the lilies of the field, how they grow; they toil not, neither do they spin: And yet I say unto you, That even Solomon in all his glory was not arrayed like one of these. Wherefore, if God so clothe the grass of the field, which to day is, and to morrow is cast into the oven, shall he not much more clothe you? . . . Take therefore no thought for the morrow: for the morrow shall take thought for the things of itself" (Matthew 6:28–30, 34).

Sudden, unexpected changes in life plans can leave one feeling emotionally stripped. In such times, these loving words from the Savior can be especially comforting. We can trust God will care for us as we place our faith in Him, one day at a time.

This lesson helped me immensely when I returned to BYU after that fateful Christmas break. I felt troubled when I thought about my future. I felt every decision I made could have extreme, unidentified eternal consequences. Just like my mom, I spent many nights alone in my bed, plagued by panic attacks and sleepless nights as I thought about all my unknowns.

I reminded myself every day, sometimes every hour, to take deep breaths and take things one step at a time. I found hope as I learned to work through uncertainty in small doses. Instead of dwelling on dramatic, fabricated scenarios where I distanced myself from everything and everybody I loved, I made lists of small, healthy decisions I could make daily to add value and meaning to my life. These decisions helped me feel empowered. I set small, short-term goals and practiced being kind to myself if I didn't reach them. Rather than allowing the uncertainty of the future to paralyze me, I reminded myself that blank pages can be a blessing.

To add a sense of meaning to my life, I made sure that every day I had at least one thing to look forward to. I signed up for extra Cosmo appearances and tried to do as many mascot hospital visits or charity foundation trips as possible. As I was engaged in meaningful activities (rather than simply staying busy), I felt energized and more worthy of love. I scheduled road trips, concerts, and hikes with friends. I felt more in control of my life when my plans worked out, and happier as I surrounded myself with people who lifted me up.

I made sure to stay close to the Lord as I dealt with feelings of uncertainty and depression. I continued to faithfully renew my covenants, serve others, and seek guidance through daily scripture study. By doing so, I have seen the Savior's promise firsthand. God has "clothed" me and given me raiment each day as I have worked to place my faith directly in Him and His plan for me. My life has confronted me with many unknowns, but as I have worked through them in increments, joy has replaced the distress that once overwhelmed me.

2. IT'S OKAY TO ASK FOR HELP.

My mom taught me this lesson by struggling to master it herself. She loved to help others, but accepting help made her feel weak and incapable, especially at a time when she wanted to feel strong and confident. From watching her, I realized that sometimes asking for help doesn't demonstrate weakness, but rather strength.

Jesus Himself taught, "Ask, and it shall be given you" (Matthew 7:7). There is power in seeking help when needed. By vocalizing our needs and recognizing our own inability to fulfill them, we demonstrate humility and reliance on the Lord.

In a discourse titled "Like a Broken Vessel," Elder Jeffrey R. Holland taught that when we stand in need, "Our Father in Heaven expects us to use all of the marvelous gifts He has provided in this glorious dispensation." He explained that we should use a combination of both spiritual and temporal resources when we have problems we cannot solve on our own. When talking specifically about depression, anxiety, and emotional affliction, Elder Holland gave the following counsel: "Seek the advice of reputable people with certified training, professional skills, and good values. Be honest with them about your history and your struggles. Prayerfully and responsibly consider the counsel they give and the solutions they prescribe" (*Ensign*, Nov. 2013).

One March morning I woke up early to go to tumbling practice with the BYU cheer squad. I had set a goal to hit a double full twisting layout by the end of the semester, and I needed more time in the gym and some technical coaching if I was going to make it happen. To my disappointment, when I walked in, I found that the tumbling practice had been replaced by a presentation by the university psychological services department.

I was already awake, and I had a few friends on the squad, so I decided to stay and sit through the PowerPoint. One of the last slides was a list of "signs" that might indicate the need to schedule a counseling session—restlessness, loss of energy, inability to focus, anxiety, panic attacks, etc. As I read through the list, I realized that ever since Christmas, I had been experiencing every single one of them. I was in a very, very low place mentally and emotionally.

The very thought of telling someone I wasn't doing okay filled me with embarrassment. Asking for help seemed unpalatable. However, from watching my mom, I had learned that sometimes it's better to seek help rather than try to solve problems alone. Later that afternoon I swallowed my pride, nervously knocked on my coach's door, and asked if Cosmo had access to the same psychological services as the cheer squad.

A few days later I stood in front of double wooden doors in the basement of the campus student center. Almost all of me wanted to turn away—to make up some busy excuse as to why I had missed my appointment, then never reply to the email asking when I wanted to reschedule. But another part of me twisted within and reminded me how tired I was—how I had been scrapping and lying and struggling and crawling, every single day.

My therapist's office was simple, but pleasant enough. There was a lumpy gray couch, pictures of travel destinations, and a shelf with hundreds of books on it. I sat awkwardly on the couch, still not sure if I was ready to open up, and talked generically about my life and family relationships.

"Why are you here, Charlie?" my therapist asked unexpectedly halfway through our third session.

"What do you mean?" I replied, my voice hesitating slightly.

"My parents had a really nasty divorce. I'm just trying to be healthy and work through it."

So far that was all I had talked about. I was scared to tell him the truth about why I needed to be there.

"Charlie, you have processed your parents' divorce very well. You've taken years to work through it and heal, and it sounds like you have great relationships with both of your parents, and all of your siblings."

I stared at a picture of a Spanish mosque that was on the shelf across from me.

"Charlie, why are you really here?"

I kept staring at the candy-cane stone arches displayed in the photograph, until finally I began to uncover part of my emotional iceberg.

"I . . . I'm not . . . I'm not normal," I started. "I'm not attracted to girls. I don't know what to do."

I spent the rest of my college career with regularly scheduled therapy appointments. Every Thursday afternoon I arrived at the double doors with trepidation, but after each counseling session I walked out with more energy and renewed self-confidence. During the week I wrote down everything that made me feel shaken, scared, broken, or anxious, then discussed it in my sessions. I was as honest as I could be. Little by little, I exposed more and more of my confusion and pain. Sharing my thoughts, experiences, and feelings with a licensed professional helped me see my life from a new perspective. He helped me work through uncertainty, move through painful experiences, and conquer insecurities I had shouldered since childhood.

Going to therapy saved me on countless occasions. It gave me practical skills I could apply to all aspects of my life and helped me overcome feelings of worthlessness and depression. I learned how to be more patient and forgiving with myself, and experienced hope I was not able to find on my own. For me, asking for help and going to therapy was not a sign of weakness, but an unparalleled strength.

3. A SHIFT IS NOT NECESSARILY A LOSS.

Loss often comes with a grief process. I watched my mom experience cycles of shock, denial, anger, bargaining, and depression when the plan she had for her future changed. However, I also watched her do her best to recognize good things that came from such a shift. There's no denying divorce was difficult for her, but she recognized silver linings wherever and whenever she could. For example, she noted improvements in her self-confidence as she became more independent. She realized she was capable of learning new skills and taking care of problems she had never encountered before. She noted how she began to see people and relationships through a new, more mature lens.

My siblings and I also recognized that a shift in our family was not necessarily a loss. By going through such difficult times together, the five of us became closer and learned how to rely on each other. We found strength as we worked to manage our evolving relationships with each of our parents. As a sibling unit, we banded together to lift and support our family.

The Old Testament recounts the story of Joseph of Egypt, who had many dramatic shifts in his life. He planned to grow up and receive the inheritance of his father, but instead his brothers threw him into a pit, faked his death, and sold him to Ishmaelite merchants as a slave. This first dramatic, and rather horrifying, life shift actually turned out to be a blessing for Joseph. Genesis 39:2 says, "The Lord was with Joseph." After being sold into

Egypt, he ended up becoming the overseer of the entire household of Potiphar, a powerful officer to the Egyptian pharaoh.

Just when things were finally going well for him, another dramatic shift caused Joseph's life plan to change completely. Due to a dramatic misunderstanding, he was thrown into prison. Again, in a singular moment, he lost everything he had worked for. But even in this dire situation, the Bible tells us, "The Lord was with him" (Genesis 39:23). His two years in prison put him in the position to interpret an important dream for the pharaoh. His prophecy that Egypt would be struck by famine came to pass, and Joseph ended up saving the country by implementing a food storage system in preparation for the famine. He became the most powerful man in Egypt and was eventually reunited with his family. Joseph's life shifts were dramatic and difficult, but they were not losses. God was with Joseph, and he was able to use his misfortunes to find ways to grow and progress.

Like Joseph and my mother, I grieved when I realized I wouldn't live the life I had always imagined for myself. When I returned to BYU after Christmas, everything seemed to be a constant reminder that I didn't fit in. Once-beloved Church lessons about the family unit were painful and hard to sit through. Many of my friends were dating, getting married, and starting families. They could move on with their lives, be parents, and live their happily-ever-afters. But me? What did I have left? I felt I had lost all hope. I felt I had lost my culture, my plans, and my very place in society.

I knew that my mom was happier when she looked for silver linings and blessings that came from living outside of the proverbial box, so I sought to do the same. Over the years I have come to see that the shift in my perceived future was not a loss but was actually a blessing to me. When I look back, I can see that the Lord has been with me the whole time, just as He was with Joseph.

When I used to imagine my future, I saw myself living in a suburb with a wife, a daughter, and a dog. Instead, I am a single gay man who travels a lot and spends free time with friends. Even though my life looks different from what I imagined, I'm still the same person. I'm the guy who listens to way too much Taylor Swift and loves to wave his arm out the car window. I embarrassingly dance in public, laugh when I'm not supposed to, and geek out over geography. I still find joy in daily scripture study, volunteer to set up chairs before baptisms, and strive to know and be close to the Savior.

I'm who I always was—just in a much better place emotionally.

Now that I accept and recognize who I am, I have more hope for the future. I believe God's view is all-seeing, all-encompassing, and far greater than my own. I know I will find courage and strength in Christ as I work to understand more about who I am, and work to unfold God's plan for me.

So, what do you do when the future you had envisioned completely dissolves?

What do you do when you break—when you spend nights staring at the ceiling and have trouble focusing? How do you cope when you feel worthless, overwhelmed, and afraid? Where do you go when life crumbles and the overpowering weight of darkness covers everything you are? What do you do when you don't want to exist anymore—when you want to disappear or just give in?

Remember you are a divine child of God with endless worth and potential. Be kind to yourself. Surround yourself with light, goodness, and uplifting friends.

Choose to live.

Move forward each day, trusting that there is light at the end of the tunnel. One day, the bleak, heavy darkness will be lifted by the sweet light of dawn. When that moment comes, you might discover your true path is even better than the one you expected.

1. Take things one day at a time.
2. It's okay to ask for help.
3. A shift is not necessarily a loss.

7

MY HAIL MARY

YOU CAN DO THIS. *She's absolutely perfect*, I reiterated to myself as I looked over at Mary in the passenger seat.

I pulled into the dusty parking lot and squeezed into a spot next to a stack of sweet, musty hay. The fields around us had suffered from the long, cold months, but today the snow was melting and the dead grass that came through looked like pure gold in the fresh sun. Horses grazed happily on a backdrop of white, snow-capped mountains, and a gentle wind blew through the canyon and waved branches on the budding trees. I rolled down my window to let the warm breeze pass over my face and eyelids.

Mary and I had basically spent the whole winter together, eternally studying accrued interest and accounts payable in the basement of the library. Today the first signs of spring were beginning to show, and we could hardly bear to stay inside any longer. Instead of going to class, we decided to treat ourselves and play hooky. For weeks we had been talking about going to a natural hot spring up the canyon, and Mary insisted today was the day. She had always been fun and spontaneous like that.

I knew I wasn't attracted to girls—it was painfully clear to me—but I was still hoping Mary might somehow be the one to break my curse. I was really struggling this semester, and being around her had helped me escape myself somehow. We had known each other since we were kids, and I loved everything about who she was. I knew almost all of her friends, enjoyed spending time with her family, and shared common interests with her by the thousands.

Other people have made it work, right? I thought to myself as we got out of my car and started up a dirt path. *Maybe I could too . . .*

Social pressure towered over me. With so many people pushing me to date, get married, and start a family, not continuing my search for a wife made me feel like I was giving up. For years I had conditioned myself to believe that accepting my sexual orientation was synonymous with quitting, so I felt guilty not trying to find a girl I could be with. I had been planning to marry in an LDS temple ever since I was a child, and I couldn't seem to completely let go of what I thought my future would be.

I decided to give it one last shot: a "hail Mary" attempt. I knew multiple stories of guys in mixed-orientation marriages (gay men who married straight women), and I resolved that if anyone could make it work, it was me. I revered women. I found them remarkable—almost superhuman. They were strong, creative, beautiful, and kind. I had never felt attracted to a girl, but maybe if I found the right one, I could turn friendship into something more?

Until now I had mostly just ghosted girls I was trying to date. In the months before Christmas, I had committed myself to going on at least three dates a week with different girls. I had been to dinners, concerts, arcades, and bowling alleys with some of the most beautiful, spiritual, well-rounded girls I'd ever met. Despite my best efforts, I didn't have any romantic feelings for any of them. When a girl would even hint at getting serious or try to "determine the relationship," I couldn't handle it. I ran away and broke off all communication, and I felt terrible about it. I didn't want to be a jerk guy who left girls hanging with no explanation, but I didn't know what else to do.

Mary and I really did have a special relationship, though, so against all warning signs I decided to try to date her. I did my best to not think about it much. I really liked spending time with her, but the thought of being in a relationship with a girl made me highly uncomfortable.

I felt better when we reached the end of the path and arrived at the hot spring. It was beautiful. A deep, warm pool of crystal-blue water lay inside a large, cavern-like room. High above, at the top of a rocky dome, a natural oculus bathed the water in brilliant sunlight. The water made a sticky echo as it lapped the sides of the rock and rippled back toward the center of the pool.

We spent the afternoon swimming in the geological spring and diving down to see if we could touch the bottom. On the way back we stopped at a homemade pie shop and talked about memories from childhood. The golden sun bounced through the canyon as we drove along, setting a perfect ending on a perfect day.

"That was definitely a lot more fun than going to class," I said, when I finally dropped her off back at her apartment.

"Oh, yeah. Let's do it again next week!" she joked as she unbuckled her seat belt and opened the door. I got out of the car and gave her a quick hug.

"I'm down," I replied with a laugh.

When I got back to my apartment a few minutes later I was bombarded by my buddies. They were all in the living room waiting for me to get back for a full report on my date.

"Bro, how'd it go?" Austin cheered as I walked through the door.

"It was fun!" I replied. "She's awesome."

"Did you kiss her?" he followed up.

All of my friends waited with eager faces for me to respond.

"Nah, you know I don't just give kisses away like that," I said, trying my best to evade the conversation while still sounding cool.

"You don't give kisses away at all," Austin replied, the excitement falling from his face.

Weeks later, once again, I got out of my car to give Mary a hug as I dropped her off at her apartment. We had spent a fantastic evening out with a group of my friends. She was engaging and witty, and I liked introducing her to new people. I still had anxiety about where things might be headed—the more I hung out with her, the more pressure I felt to date her seriously—but I really enjoyed being around her, so I tried to focus on that instead. As I pulled away from the hug, she caught my waist to keep me from leaving.

"Hey, can I ask you something?" Her voice was soft but sure.

"What's up?" I replied.

"How come you never kiss me?" she said bluntly.

We had been "unofficially" dating almost a month. I knew this conversation would come up eventually, but I still wasn't sure how to handle it. I suddenly felt nervous and on edge. My heart began beating faster as I scraped my mind for something to say.

"I've kissed you before . . ." I stumbled.

"Not really. Not, like, an actual kiss," she countered.

She was right. The few times I had kissed Mary, I had essentially turned into a fish. I knew she was beautiful—all my friends talked about was how she was way out of my league—but the thought of "actually" kissing her made me very uncomfortable. It felt unnatural and insincere. I loved her as a person, but kissing her felt very, very wrong.

As we talked, I thought about how much I cared about her. I realized if I ever wanted to make it work, I would have to get over my aversion to kissing and take the relationship to the next level. I took a few moments to muster all the fortitude I could possibly find. Then, I fought through my screaming internal conflict, pulled her closer to me, and kissed her.

While we kissed I desperately sought to feel something. I tried to swan dive into my emotions, doing everything I could to invoke some sort of romantic connection.

Anything.

Anything?

Nothing.

By the time we finished kissing I felt humiliated and dismayed. A weird combination of pity and guilt crept into my bones. Kissing her seemed to go against the very makeup of my soul. I did everything I could to remain emotionally present—to not detach myself or spiral. I wanted so badly to want her, but I felt completely empty. My conscience went off like a siren, blaring at me to run away and leave.

I couldn't just leave her, though—she was one of my best friends. I couldn't stand the thought of hurting her like I had hurt all the other girls. I had never been in this deep.

As I wrestled with my convoluted emotions, her voice pierced my eardrums.

"I really like you, Charlie," she said nervously. "I know you usually don't do serious relationships, but what if we made this exclusive? What do you think about making it official?"

Her words caught me completely off-guard. I was still dazed and disordered from the kiss. I had no idea what to say.

"Mary . . . uh . . . I just . . ." I hesitated. "I don't think this is going to work out between us," I finally spouted out stupidly.

"What? Why not?" she asked, sounding both hurt and surprised. "Is there . . . is there something wrong with me?" she asked awkwardly, with a slight edge in her voice.

"No!" I replied honestly. "Nothing at all. You're incredible, Mary. You're interesting and strong and resilient and beautiful."

"What is it, then?" she asked, bewildered by my response.

I sat in silence for a long time, lost in a storm of thoughts and emotions. Maybe some people could make a mixed-orientation relationship work, but I knew that I couldn't. Trying to force it was already hurting both of us. I felt selfish for leading her on when I knew I couldn't be who she deserved. I wanted her to have someone who loved her, who could grow with her, and who could give everything to her. No matter how much I loved and respected women, I realized I was never going to be that guy.

"I . . . I'm sorry but I think I should go," I said, feeling completely miserable. "It's late and we both have a big test tomorrow."

"Are you serious right now?" she asked.

I stared at her blankly, unable to say anything. I hated the whole situation, and I felt foolish for not knowing how to handle it in a more respectful manner.

"Okay," she said sharply as she got out of my car. "Good night, I guess. See you around."

I felt a pang in my chest, somewhat blurred by the confusion and uncertainty that fought for my emotional attention. As I drove away, I could see Mary through my rearview mirror, walking back to her doorstep alone.

8

HORSEPOWER

I OFTEN JOKE about how there are more cows than people in the town where I grew up. My earliest memories include waking up before sunrise to bottle-feed calves in the old red barn behind our house. My older sisters and I spent every weekend and every summer spreading grain, hauling hay, and herding livestock. I still credit all of our cross-country medals to the training we got while running through fields chasing cattle.

We had four horses. Izzy was grullo gray and taller than a pickup truck. He was smart and gentle and had an even gait. Mare was a mare (don't blame me for her unimaginative name). She was a beautiful, well-trained pedigree horse. Dude was a classic California boy. He was palomino blond, laid back, and loved any attention he could get. I could ride him even without a saddle.

Our last horse, however, was a different story. He had an assigned pedigree name, but his reputation quickly earned him the nickname "Buck." Due to his size, power, and instinct, for years I wasn't allowed to ride him. He was born and bred to be a headstrong cattle horse.

Buck was built like a freight train. He was powerful, and

he knew it. Even when I was old enough, for months I was too scared to even attempt riding him. The first few times I tried proved frustrating and painful. He seemed to know how scared I was, and he usually proved his dominance through defiance. I often ended up face-first in the dirt as he bolted off into the pasture, wild and unrestrained. I didn't understand why my family would keep such an incorrigible horse. I thought it would be easier if I didn't have to deal with him at all.

I must have been about as stubborn as Buck was, because after each failure I became even more determined to master him. He grew to be my horse of choice every time I got the chance to saddle up. In time, I learned that when handled properly, Buck's power and strength became valuable assets. When I figured out how to bridle him, he was easily the best horse I had ever worked with. I learned how he responded to the reins and how to control his speed. Once I knew how to channel his power, when he bolted off into the pasture, it was on my terms. We would race through open fields, working together in an exhilarating rush of speed, strength, and agility.

Ancient scripture tells us the wise counsel the prophet Alma gave to his son Shiblon. In Alma 38:12, he said, "Use boldness, but not overbearance; and also see that ye bridle all your passions, that ye may be filled with love." The phrase "bridle all your passions" shows not only Alma's maturity but also his comprehension of emotional and spiritual well-being. Alma understood that feelings and emotions are powerful, and how we deal with them has a significant effect on our ability to love.

When handled properly, a bridle allows a horse to operate at maximum efficiency. The bridle keeps both the rider and the horse safe, and ensures they become one. To bridle does not mean to forcefully restrain or suppress but to guide in a healthy way. By moving forward at my own pace, seeking a comprehensive view of my orientation, and honoring my agency, I have been able to bridle my passions and partake of Alma's beautiful promise to be filled with love.

Progress is a key element of the doctrine of Jesus Christ. Even faith, the first principle of the gospel, is a principle of action. The same Alma that counseled his son to bridle his passions also taught the importance of experimenting and acting on faith. He compared faith to the growth of a seed, and instructed that in order for our faith to grow and progress, we must actively nourish and exercise it. Robert J. Matthews, ancient scripture historian, wrote that "true faith always moves its possessor to some kind of physical and mental action; it carries an assurance of the fulfillment of the things hoped for. A lack of faith leads one to despair."

A bridle is rendered useless if a horse is not in motion. In a similar way, when I let fear of progression keep me from seeking direction regarding my orientation, I was unable to bridle my passions. I thought if I ignored my feelings I could overcome and destroy them. I worried if I accepted them, they would overcome and destroy me. This stagnant approach filled me with exasperation. I felt frustrated and confused, and I detested my same-gender attraction.

I hated myself.

One night I received a text from one of my best friends asking me if I was still awake. She explained that she was sick and wanted a priesthood blessing, and she wondered if I would be willing to help. Instead of going to her apartment to offer the blessing, I ignored her text and crumpled up on a beanbag chair in my living room. I lay there for almost an hour, internally beating myself up for being attracted to men. I wasn't able to get up and break my emotionally damaging mental cycle until one of my roommates came home and found me lying alone in the dark.

At that time, I viewed my orientation the same way I used to view Buck: annoying, frightening, and ruinous. Suppressing and punishing myself for my feelings led me to feel stuck and alone. By not moving forward or seeking heavenly answers concerning my identity, I consigned myself to marinate in my confusion and pain. My ability to serve others was diminished, and I often mentally abused myself on proverbial beanbag chairs instead of reaching out.

Thankfully, true to Alma's words, bridling my passions filled me with love. By turning to God and making spiritually calculated steps to honor who I am, I began to progress and learn more about my divine nature. I used tools I was familiar with (such as scriptures and prayer) to ask questions about who I am and how I should move forward. Sometimes answers came softly, in the form of increased feelings of peace and happiness. Other times, I received breakthrough revelation, such as the answer to my sincere prayer in the Washington D.C. Temple. As I took courageous steps forward, the love in my heart began to increase. I felt more connected to my Heavenly Parents and developed a deeper knowledge of the infinite love of the Savior. I became more understanding and forgiving of myself and stopped punishing myself for feelings I couldn't control.

I have become especially fond of the prophet King Benjamin's advice in Mosiah 4:27: "It is not requisite that a man should run faster than he has strength." Elder Dieter F. Uchtdorf expounded on this principle. He said, "The Lord doesn't expect us to work harder than we are able. He doesn't (nor should we) compare our efforts to those of others. Our Heavenly Father asks only that we do the best we can—that we work according to our full capacity, however great or small that may be" (*Ensign*, Nov. 2009). Rather than comparing myself to others, or expecting to have all the answers at once, I try to allow myself to move forward at my own pace. I'm happier when I don't put unreasonable expectations on my growth process, and instead seek to be grateful for the progress I do make.

Another way I have been able to successfully bridle my passions is by seeking a comprehensive view of my orientation. A mouth bit that is fitted improperly on a bridle can cause a horse considerable pain. I grew up in a culture where being gay was directly equated with sexual activity. Because everyone associated homosexuality directly with sex, that's where I felt I had to control my feelings. The "bit" I was using to regulate my life was improper, and it made me feel constantly out of control. I became extremely rigid and was unable to see how being gay can sometimes be a blessing.

Recently I visited a friend's congregation just north of Salt Lake City. I arrived a little late and ended up taking a spot in the very back on a metal chair in the overflow section. After the sacrament had been blessed and passed, I noticed a small girl in the row ahead of me. She had taken out a pack of art supplies and a coloring book. After coloring in her first rose, she sat and stared at her colored pencils. She looked back and forth from the pencils to the mostly blank page for a while, then scanned the room around her. I watched her, now interested in which color she would choose for the next flower. She looked back at me often, meeting my gaze. Finally, she confidently reached her hand through the back of her chair and tapped me on the knee.

"You know what color to use, don't you," she said, more of a statement than a question. She climbed through her chair and held her box of colored pencils up to my eyes.

"Will you help me decide?"

I was taken aback by her intuition and humbled by her immediate trust in me, even though I was a fully grown, male stranger. I was also really excited that she had asked for my advice, because I had been looking at the colors too, and I knew exactly which ones she should use.

"What about these two?" I suggested. "I think they would look pretty together, and they go really well with the colors you already used."

She spent the rest of the meeting in the chair next to me, and together the two of us worked to finish her coloring page of stained-glass roses. When the meeting ended, the little girl hugged my knees and ran off to her Primary class, her newly finished coloring page in hand. Her mom thanked me quickly, then went to accompany her daughter to class.

"That was amazing!" said my friend as we walked out of the overflow room into the foyer. "How does that happen?" she questioned.

"How does what happen?" I replied.

"It was like she knew you were gay!" said my friend, almost in disbelief. "She, like, read your soul and trusted you immediately."

"How could she know I was gay? She doesn't even know what that means," I countered.

"Maybe what everyone else labels as *gay* she just sees as safe, helpful, and creative," my friend replied.

For the rest of the day I thought about how the little girl saw me as safe, helpful, and creative. It reminded me that my identity holds so much more than just my sexual orientation. To me, the moment was a tender mercy that showed me I belong at church. In an environment where I sometimes feel like I don't fit in, that little girl showed me that my presence was valued and needed.

The interaction also reinforced my belief that my unique worldview allows me to connect with others in meaningful ways.

One of the greatest blessings I have seen from being gay is my natural ability to connect with and understand women. It is easy for me to respect women and see them for who they truly are, in part because of my frank inability to sexually objectify them. Being gay has also helped me develop greater appreciation and understanding for marginalized groups. I know what it's like to feel like an outsider, and as such have developed increased empathy for women, people of color, and other minorities. The same is true within a Church setting, where I empathize with people who don't fit the typical mold, such as single mothers, unmarried adults, recent converts, or people who have different political or religious views. This perspective allows me to love and serve other children of God in a unique way. While I once viewed being gay as a spiritual weakness, I now know that it can, in fact, be a strength.

I don't fully understand yet, but I also believe there is something about being gay that has influenced my creativity. Many of the best artists, musicians, dancers, and designers I know are gay. I hesitate to promote stereotypes, and can't speak for everyone, but I feel a strong correlation between my orientation and my propensity for design.

I believe all would do well to realize that being gay is not equal to sexual activity. To reduce someone to sex is dehumanizing and inappropriate, and often leads to improper judgment. The pull I feel toward the same gender is not just sexual. There are elements of companionship, compatibility, and emotional connection that make up my romantic attraction. All of these factors influence who I am and how I interact with those around me. By realizing that my orientation goes far beyond physical attraction, I have become more understanding and compassionate toward myself and others. Spiritual and cultural challenges that stem from being gay have helped me to grow dependent on the power of prayer and personal revelation as I seek to find where God needs me to fit in His earthly kingdom. I've had to work really hard to find answers, and I am stronger because of it.

Helaman 14:30 says, "Behold, ye are free; ye are permitted to act for yourselves; for behold, God hath given unto you a knowledge and he hath made you free." The freedom to navigate our own lives and make personal decisions is one of the greatest gifts that God has bestowed upon humankind. Agency allows for diversity and individuality, and feeds into the ultimate goal to progress and become. Honoring my agency has helped me connect my personal progress to my healthier views on sexual orientation, and thereby live more fearlessly.

I can't choose the way I feel, but I can choose what to do with it. It's easy to let fear and shame paint me into a corner, but I feel closer to God when I'm actively engaged in seeking heavenly guidance concerning who I am. In a discourse on agency, the prophet Jacob said, "Therefore, cheer up your hearts, and remember that ye are free to act for yourselves" (2 Nephi 10:23). Jacob indicates that rather than being stressed out and disheartened by agency, we should be thankful for it.

Once, while on a road trip with my cousin Rachel, I explained to her the fear that crept in when contemplating my future. I related the stress and pressure I felt as I observed other people in my similar situation. I had watched many of them make choices I didn't think would be healthy for me. My mind obsessed over worry that I might meet a spiritually destructive end. I explained to her how I didn't want to make any decisions that would take me down a wrong path, and how I always wanted to stay close to the Lord.

"Why are you so scared of your potential to be bad?" she asked after listening to me for a few minutes. "I mean, sure, by not doing anything you might avoid making wrong decisions, but you also cut off your ability to make right ones. Agency is a gift, Charlie. Not a curse. If you really want to stay close to God, you can't let fear paralyze you. You can't be static; you have to actively exercise your faith."

When I rode Buck, I often had acres of open field and forest ahead of me. I didn't always know the path we would take from the get-go. If I didn't like the direction we were headed, I could pull on the reins and he would change course. I used his bridle to avoid trees, sinkholes, ponds, and fences that I couldn't initially see. Each time I fell off or made a mistake, I became better prepared for the next time. In a similar way, agency allows me to change course if I don't like the direction my life is headed. I can steer and guide myself as I go, and trust that the Lord will direct my path.

Whenever I make mistakes, I can use them to learn, set boundaries, and progress. The gifts of agency and repentance mean that no one decision is ever damning or final. I take courage in that, as a child of loving Heavenly Parents, I will always have the ability to reroute if I so desire. Through Christ, repentance can be about learning, not restitution. I treasure that His Atonement allows me to use failure as a way to learn and improve.

Even though initially it seemed impossible, I'm grateful I found the courage and determination to learn how to ride Buck. If I never would have saddled up, I never would have known what it was like to gallop through an open field of freshly cut alfalfa. I never would have felt the wind on my face or seen the sunlight dance over me as it cut through leaves in the trees above.

Buck's bridle did not stifle him, but allowed him to channel his strength and power into grace and productivity. Learning how to properly guide Buck diminished my fears and replaced them with trust and admiration. By the same token, taking Alma's advice to bridle my passions—to guide them in a healthy way—has allowed me to realize considerable spiritual and emotional growth. I now understand there's a way I can honor who I am without falling into a spiritually destructive path. I am no longer scared of myself, because I no longer reduce myself to sexual orientation—I know my identity encapsulates so much more than that. By seeking the Lord's guidance to better understand who I am, I have felt much closer to God. I've seen that for me, being gay can even sometimes be one of my most sacred spiritual gifts.

As I've come to accept myself, I've realized that my spiritual strength isn't determined by how thoroughly I suppress my feelings. I have real power when I bridle them.

9

IN SPITE OF IT ALL

"I WISH YOU COULD SEE how much Jesus loves you," Sayre said earnestly between sobs. "Jesus loves you so much."

I was crying too. Between my flood of tears and the fading light of dusk, it was a wonder I could even see the road. Coming out to him had been an explosion. I had prepared my words beforehand, hoping to sound eloquent and put-together, but instead I was a blabbering, disorderly mess.

Sayre and I usually listened to high school throwback songs on the road. We talked about our friends, reminisced about performing at NBA halftime shows, and dreamed of hikes and art we wanted to see on upcoming trips. This time, however, the drive was free from loud music and regular conversation. Instead, we had a deep discussion about mercy, divine potential, and Christ's redemptive power, which allowed me to share with him my most guarded secret.

I was beginning to see a pattern—coming out to Sayre was one of the most beautiful spiritual experiences of my life. As I exposed the heaviest parts of my soul, the dark, heavy walls I felt trapped by suddenly transformed into glass. The Spirit permeated my heart and testified of the Savior's unconditional love for me. I caught a rare glimpse of my divine worth, and my faith was heightened as I connected with Sayre on a deep, vulnerable level. I was met with understanding and hope, and felt an outpouring of heavenly love.

Our eyes were dry, but still red, as we neared my grandparents' home near St. George, where we were planning to stay the night. I knew we wouldn't be done talking anytime soon, so instead of heading to their house, I pulled into an empty lot and threw the car in park. The light of day was completely gone now, and a cool blanket of night had set in on the desert around us.

As we talked, our conversation shifted to my emotional well-being. We were almost always together, and I figured Sayre could tell I hadn't been doing well. He was the one who had found me on the beanbag chair at 2:00 a.m., stuck in a spiral of self-loathing just a few months before. As I began to open up about the pain, fear, and uncertainty I had been facing, my emotions began to shift. The peace and safety I had felt as I came out to him fled, and heat began rising in my chest. Bitterness crept in as I explained to him how difficult my life was and how the cards I had been dealt didn't seem fair.

"Everyone has challenges though, right? It's not like life is really 'fair' for anyone," he said. "I mean, the gospel isn't about checking boxes or fitting in. It's about becoming a disciple of Christ. There's not really one perfect way of doing anything."

"This isn't just a challenge, though," I said to him with exasperation. "It's part of me." I let out a deep sigh, then continued, "All I want to do is stay close to God and try to figure this out, but I feel like no matter what I do, everyone will just see me as a dangerous, defective, perversion. To most people, that's all I'll ever be."

"Why do you say things like that?" he retorted, sounding defensive. "No one actually believes that."

"Yes they do. Look at this." I pulled out a file in the notes section of my phone.

For the past few months I had kept a running list of everything that Church leaders had ever said about "homosexuality." The list was comprehensive, and many of the quotes were blunt and felt vicious to me.

"Look at these quotes, Sayre." I began to read them aloud. "This one—where simply being attracted to the same sex is called a 'malady, and a detestable crime against nature.' Or this one, that says if anyone has same-sex attraction, then they haven't prayed hard enough."

I felt increasingly hurt as I read through the list. All I ever wanted was to feel close to God, but these quotes made me feel like He wouldn't want me.

"This is what people 'know' about being gay, Sayre. This is what everyone around me has been taught." I felt sullen and overwhelmed. "These were leaders. They were supposed to be helping," I cracked. My heart broke all over again as I dug into my pain.

I felt a hard shell of anger trying to envelop me, and I let it.

"They put being gay up with rape and child molestation. They accredited homosexuality to early sexual abuse, bad parenting, and unhealthy family dynamics. They suggested it could be cured with invasive therapy methods."

My anger was a boa constrictor, tightening with angst.

"So, yeah, how am I supposed to compete with that? No matter what I do, this is how people will see me," I finished.

The words spat out of my mouth. Reading through the quotes made me furious. When I was younger, I had buried myself in these words. Now, thinking about how damaging they were filled me with rage. I wanted to upheave and upturn everything in my path. I wanted to scream at everyone who had ever suggested that "homosexual tendencies" were wicked and perverted. I wanted them to know exactly what their words did to a scared, lonely boy whose soul cracked every time he read them. I wanted them to know about every sleepless night, every self-loathing thought, and every agonizing moment my hope shattered into meaningless fragments.

"Take this. Look at them!" I urged him.

"No! I don't want to look at your list," Sayre replied, sounding repulsed. "How often do you read this?" he asked.

I didn't say anything. I sat there, slightly embarrassed. Spite and bitterness had become an addiction. Like it was a drug, I returned to my phone every night to read negative commentaries about my church and its history with the LGBTQ community. I let the degrading words of strangers saturate my mind and fill me with hate. I obsessed over reading about Church policy, retracted statements, and especially this list of comments from Church General Authorities.

"A lot," I finally replied.

"Why do you waste your time wallowing in this? Do you really want to hold on to this forever? Do you really want to . . . to become obsessed with what other people might think?"

Now I was boiling. How could he not understand? These quotes had ruined my life!

"I grew up reading this, Sayre!" I countered. "I grew up *believing* it. These words gutted me! They ripped my soul in two. I can't just pretend like it never happened," I snapped.

I was so mad my vision was beginning to blur.

"Do you believe anything in this list is true?" he asked.

"No, none of it," I replied angrily.

"Does any of it make you better?" His voice remained steady and calm.

"I . . ."

I thought for a moment. In the past the quotes had always made me feel sad, broken, and desperate. Now, years later, they made me writhe in pain and bitterness.

"No . . ." I replied quietly.

"Charlie, you're one of the happiest people I know. Why do you want to be spiteful? This has poisoned you for years, and will keep poisoning you until you decide to stop."

I stared at him through the darkness, lost for words to say.

"It doesn't matter to me what other people think, or what other people have said. I grew up in the same church as you, and I see you for who you are. You are virtuous. You are good. I trust your goodness. Other people will see that as well. I can't imagine how hard this must be for you—I feel unworthy to even try—but if you keep looking for reasons to hate, you are going to find them. Maybe you'll feel powerful and validated for a little while, but eventually you'll end up vindictive and bitter."

He continued, "If you really want things to change—if you really want this cycle to stop—you can't fight hate with hate. You can't sit in your bitterness. You have to forgive. It might take everything you have. It might be the hardest cross you'll ever have to carry, but you have to forgive or you'll never be able to heal. You have to have faith that others will recognize you for who you truly are, not based on outdated perceptions. You have to find a way to let it go, or you'll never truly be happy."

I didn't know if I would be able to let it go. I knew things were changing. I knew the Church was making progress, especially in the past few years, but the many attempts to increase understanding seemed so feeble compared to past rhetoric.

"Sayre, I . . ."

Was it possible to someday be at peace with this? Could I ever work through the pain from feeling mistreated and systematically excluded? How could I let it go? I wasn't even sure I wanted to. It would be so much easier to hold on to my anger.

But Sayre was right.

None of the quotes I had copied down felt true to me, and reading them was poison. I thought about how I had spent every night letting them seep through me like a cancer, causing me to brim with hate. The words were shackles, chaining me to resentment.

I remembered Christ's lasts words, as He suffered on a bloody cross after being mercilessly tormented and beaten: "Father, forgive them; for they know not what they do" (Luke 23:34).

Could it be that the men who said these things didn't fully understand what they were saying? What if, at the end of the day, they were imperfect humans like me, who sometimes let fear or prejudice influence what they said? Was I really going to hold that against them forever, even at the expense of my own happiness?

No.

If Jesus could forgive those who drove nails into His wrists, maybe I could forgive those whose words had driven nails into my spirit.

I stared out the window for a few minutes while both of us sat in silence. The tension was beginning to subside, and I felt more in control of my emotions.

"You're right," I said out loud as I reached to unlock my phone.

I backed out of the file, slid my finger across the screen, and tapped on the little red trash icon. The list disappeared.

"Think about us just thirty minutes ago," Sayre said. "That power . . . that love . . . *that's* the gospel. *That's* truth, you know?"

The feeling I'd had when I came out to Sayre was one of peace and hope. It was the same one I had felt often during my missionary service. It came each time I baptized someone or gave a priesthood blessing of healing or comfort. It was the feeling that burned in my chest as an eleven-year-old, when I knelt in my closet to say a heartfelt prayer after finishing the Book of Mormon for the first time. It was how I felt when I prayed with my family and when I first held my nieces and nephews.

"I'm here for you no matter what you do," Sayre continued. "I just don't want you to focus on the bad so much that you overlook the good. I would hate to see you throw everything away just because some things don't sit right."

"I'm too good for that, huh?" I said.

"We both are," he confirmed.

I looked back down at my phone. At the bottom of the screen was another icon, a clear page with a pencil. I tapped it and a blank note appeared. Sayre waited in the passenger seat while I took time to ponder and type out a list of new goals:

- Study how to acknowledge pain without letting it turn into bitterness or hate.
- No more negativity.
- Pray for those who might ignorantly hurt you.
- Try to be more patient and forgiving.
- Dedicate time spent reading old quotes to reading uplifting material.
- Study and pray to know that the prophet and apostles are called of God.

I finished typing and set my phone facedown on the middle console. It felt good to have something positive to replace the old note I had deleted. Moving forward, I would look to the future, not bury myself in the past.

We sat in a comfortable silence for a few minutes, looking out into the night. I said a quiet prayer of gratitude for Sayre. I knew my Heavenly Parents were watching out for me. The peaceful feeling was back, bringing new hope with it.

Now that the emotional roller coaster had come to an end, I was exhausted. I wondered if Granny was worried that we hadn't made it in yet, and whether or not she had any cornbread. I flipped on the headlights, put the car in gear, and started driving.

"You know . . . you're a lot easier to understand when you're not a blubbering wreck," I said with a grin.

"You're one to talk!" Sayre shot back.

Both of us laughed as I drove ahead, leaving my list of quotes where they had come from: deep in the past.

Clouds hung low on the mountain, but I could still make out the massive block Y that sat about halfway up. It was as if a giant typewriter had stamped it into place. I made my way past the glass exterior of the library, breathing in the crisp November air. The ground held snowy evidence that winter was approaching. Half-melted pockets of white ice made the chrysanthemums that dotted the flowerbeds look even more vibrant.

Just moments ago campus had seemed largely empty, but now that class was out, hurried footsteps and animated conversations spilled from the buildings to the concrete walkways around me. Usually students moved like bees, darting every which way in ones and twos, but it was Tuesday morning, which meant we all moved in the same direction. I followed the crowd, which traveled steadily across campus, winding its way up the spiral ramp of a pedestrian walkway and into the Marriott Center.

Once there I paused at the top of the arena. Over the weekend I had been down on the basketball court, giving high fives in the Cosmo suit and doing flips for screaming fans. The glossy wooden floors were now completely covered in black fabric, and a wide oak podium sat in the middle of the floor. I stood at the top of the stairs and scanned the crowd. After a few seconds I saw Sayre standing and waving with both hands from down below. Sam was sitting by him, with an empty spot for me in between.

They must have gotten here super early, I thought. They were sitting much closer than we usually did for BYU devotionals, and this one was sure to be packed.

It seemed fitting that I would be sitting between them for this. Just over a month before, the three of us had been in our living room watching general conference on a television set. It had been my first conference since deleting the notes on my phone, and I had spent months preparing for it. I read and listened to countless talks and sought to hear counsel from the Lord's anointed with an open mind and a forgiving heart. It made a big difference. When it was time to sustain the prophet and General Authorities of the Church, I stood from my spot on the couch between Sayre and Sam and confidently raised my arm to the square.

Now I walked down the stairs, maneuvered over the backpacks and jackets that covered the floor, and squeezed in between my buddies. A hush moved through the Marriott Center. Beginning at the far end of the arena, students began to respectfully stand as President M. Russell Ballard walked out from the tunnel and onto the floor.

"I'm pretty excited," Sam whispered to me. "This is the first time I've heard a General Authority speak in person."

The entire room teemed with reverence and anticipation. After a short prayer and a special musical number, the devotional began.

President Ballard announced that his talk would follow a "Q&A" format and started off with a quote from Joseph Smith:

"The fundamental principles of our religion [are] the testimony of the apostles and prophets concerning Jesus Christ, 'that he died, was buried, and rose again the third day, and ascended up into heaven'; and all other things are only appendages to these, which pertain to our religion" (*Teachings of the Prophet Joseph Smith*, 121).

The Spirit spoke truth to my heart as he recited the words. I recalled a document my mom had framed proudly on the wall of my childhood home, titled "The Living Christ: The Testimony of the Apostles." It was a declaration of the divine role of the Savior. Their united testimony spoke powerfully of the birth, life, ministry, and death of Jesus Christ. It testified that the Savior atoned for the sins and sorrows of the world, was crucified on Calvary's cross, and rose triumphantly on the third day. It declared that the Savior lives today, that He watches over us, and that He will return again to the earth. At the bottom of the document were the signatures of the then-current First Presidency and Quorum of the Twelve Apostles of the Church to seal their witness.

I considered how throughout my life, hearing testimonies from prophets and apostles had influenced my own testimony of the Savior. Their words had shaped my understanding of the divine mission of Jesus Christ ever since I was a child. I knew the Savior better because they knew Him and were willing to share their strong, personal witness.

President Ballard cracked a grandfatherly joke, expressed a sincere desire to give proper counsel to those in attendance, and reinstated his divine calling to "build up the Church, teach the doctrine of Christ, and help those in need of help." I was impressed by his humility, because before he began answering questions he gave a caveat that, although he was a "General Authority," he was not an "authority in general." He noted that in life, some issues or concerns may require expert help.

The room was quiet as he spoke, save the occasional flip of paper or scratch of a pen. He presented each question, then followed up with a well-thought-out answer. I was sitting back in my chair and listening calmly until the third question caught me completely off-guard.

"What message do you have for LGBT young single adults?"

I snapped to attention, instinctively leaning forward.

It was my question—the one I desperately needed an answer to. It was the question I had faithfully submitted into every single Church "question and answer" queue for the past two years. My stomach dropped and began a dance between nervousness and excitement. I felt muscles tense all over my body as President Ballard opened his mouth and began to speak.

"I want anyone who is a member of the Church who is gay or lesbian to know I believe you have a place in the kingdom," he began.

Relief flooded my being. I had been trying so desperately to keep faith that I had a place in God's kingdom. Hearing those words from an Apostle of the Lord calmed a sea that had raged in my heart.

He continued, "I recognize that sometimes it may be difficult for you to see where you fit in the Lord's Church, but you do."

I felt seen. Not only was he addressing my concerns, but he was recognizing the pain and struggle I often dealt with as a gay member of the Church.

"We need to listen to and understand what our LGBT brothers and sisters are feeling and experiencing. Certainly we must do better than we have done in the past so that all members feel they have a spiritual home where their brothers and sisters love them and where they have a place to worship and serve the Lord" (BYU devotional, Nov. 14, 2017).

An Apostle of God was publicly addressing my deepest concerns. The initial question had been specific only to LGBT single adults, but President Ballard took it a step further. He called on *all* members of the Church to do better than they had in their past treatment toward LGBT individuals. He recognized the Church's historical lack of understanding, and the othering effect it may have had. Now, he was counseling all to create spaces where LGBT members of the Church could exercise their faith in a loving, welcoming environment.

Sam nudged me with his shoulder and flashed me a toothy grin. Sayre followed suit and elbowed me in the ribs.

As he continued with questions, President Ballard touched on many more of my concerns, including the Church's stance on the protection of LGBT civil rights and how to heal when Church leaders hurt your trust. It felt comforting to know my presence in the Church wasn't overlooked, and neither were my pains. For the first time in a long time, I felt like I was swimming with the current, not against it.

Since deleting the notes on my phone and setting more positive goals, I had been feeling increased love for Church leaders, more comfortable at church, and much closer to the Savior. However, *this* was the moment that proved to me Sayre really had been right. The final strands of healing rushed through me. I could see that Church General Authorities were praying for understanding and doing better to create space for believers with different identities or orientations. I was finally moving out of the painful confusion and misunderstandings of the past, and it felt like they were too.

Hope smiled brightly before me.

10

REUSABLE YARN

MY CHILDHOOD BEDROOM had a large, west-facing window that hung between two towering bookshelves. As it once served as my great-grandmother's library, the shelves were filled with novels, encyclopedias, paintings, and other treasures. In the afternoon, when the sun had crossed into the back half of the sky, light would come through the blinds and cast a block of stripes on the carpet. I loved to lie there on the floor, surrounded by timeworn books and thick encyclopedias. I spent hours reading about exotic animals, ancient civilizations, and faraway lands.

Sunday afternoons in my room were my favorite. I would climb up my bedpost, remove an old globe from its place, and set it on the floor to study. My sisters often joined me for one of my favorite games: "Where will Charlie serve his mission?" One of them would spin the globe while I closed my eyes and ran my fingertip up and down the smooth, spherical edges. Wherever my finger was when the globe stopped spinning indicated where I would serve. We laughed for hours, imagining me crawling through the thick jungles of Brazil or wrapped up in a fur parka on the streets of Moscow.

Whenever they retired for Sunday naps, I faithfully climbed

back up the bedpost to replace the globe, then picked out a new book to read. The entire right shelf was filled with Sunday material. I spent hours on the warm carpet, accompanied by the earthy smell and rustling noise of old, amber pages. There were enough scripture study helps and Church history albums that I could read for years and never finish them all, though I did my best to try.

Throughout my childhood, faith was a beautiful feeling that grew easily. The more I studied, the more I believed. I centered myself around being a member of The Church of Jesus Christ of Latter-day Saints. Everything always seemed to make sense for me. I felt I knew exactly where I fit in the grand scheme of things.

My long-awaited missionary assignment was a far cry from the exotic places I had once imagined in the globe game, but I witnessed firsthand the power of God as I taught the restored gospel of Jesus Christ. I saw lives change, and I was proud that my church was the vehicle for truth. I came home from my mission with a deeper conviction than ever before, excited to continue my path as a faithful Church member.

I'm not sure I can adequately describe how it felt to be turned completely upside down.

I had always seen my future in the Church through the lens of being married to a woman and raising a family. When that lens shattered, the tapestry of my faith began to unravel. While I once was a hopeful little boy that sang solos in the Primary music program, I suddenly felt like a stranger to my own religion. Things that had never bothered me now clawed at the forefront of my mind. I felt overwhelmed by Church culture and how excluded it sometimes made me feel. Skepticism crept into even the strongest parts of my testimony. I loved my church, and wanted to be there, but sometimes I felt like an alien in the pew. I felt voiceless, misunderstood, and isolated.

I longed to be a child again. I ached to read scripture stories on the floor of my bedroom and feel like everything made sense, but feeling rejected by my own tribe brought a pain I'd never known. My soul craved safety, refuge, and support, but I didn't know where to find it. I felt frustrated and hurt by Church leaders and systematically excluded, like I was always on the outside looking in. It seemed it would be so easy to fit in anywhere other than the church I was raised in. Still, stepping away didn't feel right. Being a member of the Church meant everything to me. I couldn't imagine my life without it. I couldn't envision a world where I wasn't active in my faith. But what was I supposed to do with my unraveling testimony?

I remember one day sitting cross-legged in my grandma's living room in Canada watching her crochet while she told stories about her childhood to our family. Her expert hands wove the crochet hook in and out of yarn at lightning speeds. My young mind was fascinated by the way a single strand of yarn could transform into anything she desired.

Later that evening while everyone else was in the kitchen, I snuck back into the living room. I planned to sit in Grandma's chair and try to crochet, just like she did. I grabbed a shiny hook, hoisted my little body onto the recliner, and reached down to pick up the cloth she had been stitching. I pulled and pulled on the yarn, but the cloth wasn't coming to me. It took several moments before I realized that as I pulled, the cloth was unraveling. I was horrified! My grandma had worked so hard to make the cloth, and all that was left were a few stitched rows and a pile of tangled yarn.

"Grandma . . ." I said awkwardly a few minutes later as I presented her with the crumpled mess of yarn, "I'm so sorry. I destroyed your cloth."

I looked up at her, sad and regretful.

"Oh, it's not destroyed—it just looks a little different than it did before! That yarn is as good as it ever was," she sang.

"But all of the work you did was wasted!" I countered.

"It wasn't wasted at all," she replied happily. "I got some good practice in, didn't I? Who knows—I might even do a better job the next time around."

My grandma saw worth in the unraveled yarn and was confident in her ability to rebuild it into something even more beautiful. She was grateful for her past experience, and excited to creatively move forward, one row at a time. Years later, adopting her positive attitude helped me address my unraveling faith. I resolved to push against the "all or nothing" mentality that suggested my convictions had been ruined beyond repair and work with the "yarn" I still had. I knew re-stitching might take serious effort, but my life had given me a lot of good practice.

In Matthew chapter seven, Jesus recounts a short parable about two men who built houses. The "wise man" built his house on a rock. When "the rain descended, and the floods came, and the winds blew, and beat upon that house," it stood firm. It didn't collapse or wash away because it was built on a sure foundation. The "foolish man," however, built his house upon the sand. When the rain, wind, and storms came, the house washed away (Matthew 7:24–26).

I noticed a common theme in people who had experienced spiritual dilemmas. Many let their beliefs wash away from them, and subsequently didn't seem to know what their true values or boundaries were. I realized if I didn't take active ownership of my faith, the same thing could easily happen to me. I didn't want my beliefs or my moral compass anywhere near a sandy foundation.

I decided to anchor them, to "tie a knot" so they wouldn't be affected by any untangling doubts.

To fortify my core values, I asked myself:

- All things aside, who do I want to be?
- What standards do I want to live by?
- What lifestyle choices bring meaning to my life?

To anchor my core beliefs, I referred to questions I had used often as a missionary:

- Do I believe that God is my Eternal Father?
- Do I believe Jesus Christ is the Son of God, my Savior and Redeemer?
- Do I believe in the Restoration of the gospel through the Prophet Joseph Smith?
- Do I believe in repentance, covenants, and the importance of taking the sacrament?
- Do I value prayer and scripture study?
- Am I living in a way that allows me to receive and act on personal revelation?

Through examining my values and core doctrinal beliefs, I reinforced my convictions in the sure foundation of Christ. As a bonus, I found some really good reasons for living the way I do. Cementing my moral compass helped me regain a sense of control and gave me confidence in my personal integrity. Solidifying my core beliefs kept me grounded in the Savior and gave me increased faith that I could overcome my doubts. Once I went back to these basics, I felt much more capable of responsibly addressing the parts of my religious experience that caused me confusion.

When Russell M. Nelson became President of the Church, he gave a powerful discourse on personal revelation. He said,

"If Joseph Smith's transcendent experience in the Sacred Grove teaches us anything, it is that the heavens are open and that God speaks to His children." He emphasized how the boy Joseph's experience set a pattern for us to follow: to directly seek God for guidance on spiritual questions. President Nelson continued, "In like manner, what will your seeking open for you? What wisdom do you lack? What do you feel an urgent need to know or understand? Follow the example of the Prophet Joseph. Find a quiet place where you can regularly go. Humble yourself before God. Pour out your heart to your Heavenly Father. Turn to Him for answers and for comfort" (*Ensign*, May 2018).

I started there—by asking God. I fasted, studied, planned, and wrote down specific questions. Then, I prayed.

As I sought understanding, I realized that focusing on the Church only as a religious institution had caused me to overlook why I even went in the first place. Rather than letting my perceptions get in the way of my ability to connect with God, I tried to remember that the Lord's Church is the earthly carrier for the gospel of Christ. I began to view the Church's structure as a spiritual framework. Using that framework, which gave me access to the words of a living prophet, the ability to renew my covenants, a faith community, and an array of spiritual tools, helps me separate Church culture from doctrine. Meaningful conversations with faithful friends and family also became an important part of my spiritual progress. This tool-based, more home-centered approach to religion has led me to healthier views on the gospel.

Serving within the Church helped my heart heal. As I did my best to magnify my callings and be charitable toward others, I realized I wasn't as isolated as I sometimes imagined, and my presence could actually be very useful. People came to me with struggles or doubts, and I was able to help them using my unique perspective as a gay member. Actively choosing to serve within the Church and minister to other members taught me what it really means to build Zion. Even though I felt different, I could still be "of one heart and one mind" (Moses 7:18). I feel reassured knowing that no matter my orientation, I can always serve others and be a disciple of Christ.

Studying the New Testament taught me the word *church* doesn't just refer to an institution, but to the body of Christ as a whole. With that in mind, I began to notice that in many ways, my church is at the forefront of equality. There are groups of faithful members meeting in bakeries before Pride parades, offering safe support and visibility to LGBTQ youth. There are unwavering Young Women leaders who teach girls about their inherent value and the importance of female voices. There are steadfast parents building righteous homes, teaching their children to treat all equally, regardless of race, gender, identity, nationality, or creed. There are Church leaders directing large-scale humanitarian efforts, and tithing funds support marginalized and impoverished people throughout the world. As I recognize the incredible ways that the Church of Jesus Christ serves others, I can't help but want to stay part of it.

Prophetic counsel helps me when my personal feelings seem to conflict with what Church leaders have said. In a September 2019 discourse titled "The Love and Laws of God," President Russell M. Nelson declared, "My dear brothers and sisters, I plead with you to seek earnestly a confirmation from the Spirit that what I [tell] you is true and is from the Lord. He has declared that we may seek knowledge from heaven and expect to receive it: 'If thou shalt ask,' the Lord promised, 'thou shalt receive revelation upon revelation, knowledge upon knowledge.' Ask your Heavenly Father if we truly are the Lord's apostles and prophets. Ask if we have received revelation on this and other matters" (BYU devotional, Sept. 17, 2019).

If I ever feel unsure about a Church statement, that's what I do. I ask God if following the specific counsel from my leaders will lead me down a healthy, correct path. When I receive spiritual confirmation of their guidance, I consider it a double witness and go all in. If I feel a teaching or remark still generates friction for me, I pray for patience and understanding. Answers don't always come quickly, which requires me to sit in a conflicting space for a time. While I do, I seek to recognize all the good I can find and do everything I can to ensure that what I don't understand never keeps me from connecting with the Savior.

This teaching by Elder D. Todd Christofferson helps me: "It should be remembered that not every statement made by a Church leader, past or present, necessarily constitutes doctrine. It is commonly understood in the Church that a statement made by one leader on a single occasion often represents a personal, though well-considered, opinion, not meant to be official or binding for the whole church" (*Ensign*, May 2012).

This reminds me of President Ballard's comment that General Authorities are not "authorities in general," and of the deleted list of quotes I once kept on my phone. Though the content from those quotes is still sometimes a source of conflict for me, reflecting on Elder Christofferson's words often helps me find peace in that conflicting space.

I consider how, many times, Church leaders are required to provide counsel within the context of society's dominant culture. I sometimes think about society's perspective in regard to homosexuality in previous generations: to those with limited exposure and education, being gay was thought to be a choice, and to many, being gay was synonymous with a culture of addiction, sickness, and immorality. I also consider how thought patterns have changed in the past few decades—how my generation finds value in recognizing spectrums, while historically most issues were predominantly viewed as "black and white."

With this in mind, I can see how, maybe, what some Church leaders have said in years past was their best personal attempt to address the harmful culture they saw around them. Perhaps it was their way of trying to protect members of the Church from any dangers they associated with being gay. I don't defend the destructive content of the quotes, but I can trust that the pain inflicted was not intentional.

I believe the prophet and apostles are inspired and called of God, but I also recognize they are still human. I think Mormon must have understood this concept when he said, "Condemn me not because of mine imperfection, neither my father, because of his imperfection, neither them who have written before him; but rather give thanks unto God that he hath made manifest unto you our imperfections, that ye may learn to be more wise than we have been" (Mormon 9:31). Despite any shortcomings they may have, I sincerely believe these leaders are doing their best to direct and lead the Savior's global Church as He would have them lead it.

2 Nephi 28:30 says, "For behold, thus saith the Lord God: I will give unto the children of men line upon line, precept upon precept, here a little and there a little; and blessed are those who hearken unto my precepts, and lend an ear unto my counsel, for they shall learn wisdom; for unto him that receiveth I will give more." My questions have never been answered all at once, but through the gift of the Holy Spirit, the Lord has always given me what I need when I'm ready for it. Sometimes answers have changed or developed as I have discovered more about who I am, but little by little I have been able to find answers for me.

A while back I felt weighed down by a particular question that I couldn't seem to find an answer to. I was living in New York City, and the busy, chaotic environment around me seemed to amplify my need for direction. As I was searching for answers, I felt prompted to turn to the scriptures. I realized that, because I had felt like asking questions about my orientation was off-limits for so long, I had never really studied the Book of Mormon through the lens of being an openly gay disciple of Christ. I wasn't initially sure if it would work—could the Book of Mormon really help me answer a bold, complex question about being gay?

That night I sent a message to the missionaries requesting a "pass-along" copy of the Book of Mormon. After the sisters brought it to me the next day at church, I went home and wrote my specific question on the cover page. I resisted the urge to write an easier, more watered-down version, and instead copied my question exactly as it was in my mind. I set a month-long goal to read the entire book through the lens of this personal question, and resolved to record any answers that came to me.

I've read the Book of Mormon many times throughout my life, but this was the first time I read it with true acknowledgment and appreciation of who I really am. I spent hours in Central Park, pen in hand, highlighting scriptures and recording impressions. It was liberating to move away from the rote, restrictive mindset I usually had when studying the scriptures. Instead, I studied with a clearly defined purpose and a passion to find answers.

I couldn't put it down. I read it on the subway, in taxicabs, and even on my lunch breaks. I gave myself the freedom to write and mark all over the fresh copy given to me by the missionaries, and I carried it with me everywhere I went.

A few weeks later, while sitting on a rocky outcrop in the middle of Central Park, I finished reading the last page. I looked around and saw that I was alone, a rarity in Manhattan, so I decided to take the familiar invitation in Moroni 10:4–5 right then and there. I knelt down and asked God if what I had read was true. After saying "amen," I went through the whole book, page by page, to look over notes I had made. I marveled at how the words of ancient prophets, written thousands of years ago, had given both practical and spiritual advice to a modern gay man in New York City. On the final page, I repeated the original question, then wrote down the answers I had received throughout the course of my experiment. As I did, the Spirit testified to me that the Book of Mormon is true, and that it was written for our day. Since then, I have completed similar experiments for other questions I've had about my life, my family, and my identity. Each time I put in spiritual work and seek for God's answers without fear or hesitation, I receive guidance, no matter how impossible my questions may seem.

When Jesus came to earth, He fulfilled the law of Moses and taught a "higher law," one based on love, personal revelation, and moral responsibility. The parameters of the law of Moses helped lay a groundwork for believers, but the higher law showed that faith truly lives when it's released from the static restraints of legalism. Faith grows when it is used to navigate precarious realms of ambiguity. Some of the strongest examples of faith have come from believers who followed the Spirit into enigmatic new territory. Peter daringly walked on water, ancient Nephites buried weapons in the midst of a war, and early Mormon pioneers crossed the plains to establish Zion. Like the law of Moses, the faith I developed as a child gave me a strong foundation to navigate the more complicated spiritual landscapes I face as an adult. My faith can be dynamic, scrappy, and brave new territory because I have a strong groundwork that has prepared me well.

I'm young, and I still have a lot of questions, but I know God imparts wisdom to all who earnestly and faithfully seek answers. As I continue to be an engaged believer, Heavenly Father continues to teach me. Through introspection, study, and prayer, I have gained deeply personal revelation regarding my divine identity, and I feel God has shared things with me that are just for me. Moreover, I recognize that many questions may not be answered for me in this life. In a recent general conference address, President Dallin H. Oaks even said, "There is so much we do not know that our only sure reliance is to trust in the Lord and His love for His children" (*Ensign*, Nov. 2019). I don't have it all figured out, but I do know that God loves me. I trust He has a plan for me.

Some people might think I'm crazy, but I'm proud to be a member of The Church of Jesus Christ of Latter-day Saints. I cherish the sacred promises I have made to follow the gospel of Jesus Christ and build the kingdom of God. I know being gay means I will probably always have to grapple with spiritual complexity, but so far, the wrestle has made me stronger. Whether male or female, black or white, gay or straight, gospel truth resonates, because all are children of God. I have many unknowns, but both the Lord *and* His called servants have assured me that there is a place for me in His Church. My faith outweighs my fears, and my desires outweigh my doubts.

All in all, I'm grateful to know my testimony is like the yarn from my grandma's cloth—I can always stitch new rows in the fabric of my faith.

11

LOCKER-ROOM TALK

MY HOT BREATH bounced off the rubber muzzle, leaving a continuous layer of condensation around my mouth. I could taste the faint chemical sting of eye black melting from my eyelids and running down my face. *This game is insane!* I thought. It had been over three hours, and the Cougars were now in their third overtime. I doubted anyone had ever been in the suit this long. Usually by now I would have taken a few breaks, but I couldn't stand to not be in a crowd that had this much energy.

During the next time-out I quickly ran to a custodial closet and ripped the mask off my head. Heat rose from the layers of clothing on my chest and I took a few glorious gasps of unrestricted air. As I downed my second water bottle, the sound of the buzzer echoed through the hallway. *Oof. Time to go*, I thought. I chucked the bottle in the trash and took one last deep breath before shoving my head back into the humid mass of rubber, padding, and fur.

Seeing through the cougar mask was like looking through two straws. I padded down the slick concrete hallway and energetically jumped around fans who were returning from the concession stand, making sure not to trip over any children on my way. The announcer's deep voice grew louder and louder as I approached the court.

"Cosmo, will you take a selfie with us?" called a voice from behind.

I turned around to see a mother with three small kids. I brought my hands to my cheeks, dramatically showing excitement like a character in a Saturday morning cartoon. With a few steps and a front handspring, I made it over to where they were standing. Her children waved at me nervously, enthusiastic smiles on their faces. I gave each of the girls a high five, and the little boy playfully wrapped his arms around my legs. My leather gloves squeaked as I took his mom's phone to snap a picture of us all together. Inside the mask I flashed a big, goofy smile—I had the best job in the world.

"Thanks, Cosmo!" she said with appreciation as I returned the phone. "We love you!"

I flashed a Y sign with my right hand as I ran on, then turned the corner back to the arena. I pushed open the double wooden doors, and a boisterous crowd came into my thin line of vision. The stands were absolutely packed with screaming fans, decked completely in royal blue. The energy was electric.

Heavy fur pulled against me as I threw my body into a series of flips. The roar of the crowd became increasingly loud when they saw me flying through the air.

"Will you marry me, Cosmo?" asked a girl after I jumped over the railing and landed in the student section. I gave her a comical shoulder shrug and everyone around us broke into laughter. Inside the mask I couldn't help but roll my eyes and grin. *I guess you can't blame a girl for trying!* I thought with a quiet laugh.

Anticipation was high as the final moments of the game were quickly approaching. BYU was down by one point. *If we score this possession, we could take it home!* I thought excitedly as I led the entire student body in one final cheer. Even though everyone was screaming as loud as they could, they all seemed to be holding their breath.

"Come on. Come on. Come on," repeated the guy standing next to me.

The ball went up.

Everyone went quiet.

No . . .

The whole crowd looked as if they had just been punched in the gut. The opposing team had scored, and just like that the game was over.

I suddenly felt sick. Now that my adrenaline was gone, I felt sluggish and dizzy. I moved through the horde of people, seeing nothing but a blur between the mass of blue shirts and the golden hardwood floors. I needed to get out of the suit—I had been wearing it for almost four hours.

Safe in the locker room a few minutes later, I tore the mask off my head once again. I looked in the mirror. My skin was blotchy and red and was discolored by the melted eye black that was smudged all over my face. My hair was matted down and stuck out in a bizarre pattern. I slowly peeled the suit from my sweaty skin and left it in a messy pile while I lay panting on the cold floor.

After about fifteen minutes I got up, organized the suit, and headed over to the showers. I could already feel soreness setting in from the jumps and flips I had done. The water felt cool and rejuvenating as it rushed over me, infusing my muscles with more life.

Once I was clean, I moved over to my locker to put on fresh, dry clothes. While I sat to put on my socks, I noticed noise coming from a few rows down. The team must have come in while I was in the shower. I could hear them opening their lockers, and I imagined them untying their shoes with sunken shoulders. *Man, I bet that was a tough loss*, I thought. *They should be proud of themselves, though. They killed it tonight.* I considered breaking protocol and going over to congratulate them in person.

The abrupt slam of a locker made me jump.

"That was so gay!" yelled a voice, loudly.

I froze. The word hung in the air like a knife.

You're fine, I reassured myself. *They aren't talking about you. Nobody knows you are gay—nobody even knows you are here.*

The team started into a tense conversation. They brutally talked about different plays from the game and how upset they were with the results. I sat and listened for a few minutes, ultimately resolving to leave and not say anything to them. I tried to be as quiet as I could while I slid on my shoes and zipped the Cosmo suit securely into its bag.

"You know," said one of the guys, "I bet we'd have a better season if it wasn't for those stupid faggot-lovers."

"What do you mean?" asked another voice.

"Didn't you hear? People are saying the reason we didn't get into a better conference is because of some gay advocacy crap. I guess a bunch of pansies got mad and started a petition since BYU doesn't cater to homos."

"No way? That's the dumbest thing I've ever heard," the voice replied.

"I know. Bunch of LGBTQ-XYZ losers. I wish there was a way they would all just die off."

I stood there by my open locker, shaking. I couldn't listen to their conversation anymore. I shut the locker door and broke through the exit as fast as I could.

12

FRESH PERSPECTIVE

THE J. PAUL GETTY Museum in Los Angeles sits boldly over the hills of Santa Monica. The modern building boasts a myriad of fountains and soaring terraces that provide 360-degree views of the surrounding valley and hills. Inside, Western art from the Middle Ages to the present is displayed. Among my favorite pieces housed in the museum is a small collection of paintings by Claude Monet. The first time I saw a Monet was there at the Getty. I rushed into the room, beyond excited to finally see my favorite artist's works in real life. I turned the corner and came face-to-face with the first painting on display.

When I looked at it from up close, it appeared almost slovenly. Disordered blots of color bled into each other. The hues mixed together to create dirty purples, pallid grays, and rusty browns. It didn't make sense to me. There I stood, in front of a masterwork by the pioneer of French Impressionism—one of the most acclaimed artists to ever live—and it was . . . ugly?

As I backed away, however, a picture began to appear. The mottled colors reconstructed, and I visualized line, shape, and form. The blotchy, ugly colors soon revealed the facade of a beautiful cathedral. Shadows played upon the lower half of the building, while the spires bathed in the fresh, golden light of sunrise. To my surprise, the overall painting was a milky blue color. I was amazed by the way the painted canvas presented light and perspective. The stone walls of the cathedral seemed to dance in the suffused light of morning. What I originally saw as an unsightly crash of colors actually turned out to be a masterpiece. *The Portal of Rouen Cathedral in Morning Light* became one of my favorite paintings from that point on.

This experience taught me an important lesson on perspective. Looking at the big picture allowed me to appreciate how each muddled blotch of color came together to create a beautiful image. Just like with a Monet painting, when we focus too much on one aspect of our lives, sometimes we see ourselves as a dirty clash of colors instead of the masterpiece that we are.

I wrote in a journal every day throughout my missionary service, and continued the habit when I returned home. By the end of my first year back at BYU, I was thriving. I had been accepted into a competitive business program and was pursuing a second major in Spanish. I landed an exciting job working with my favorite humanities professor and started coaching youth at a tumbling gym. I received both academic and athletic scholarships, visited multiple new countries, and made amazing, spontaneous friends that would skip school to go hiking with me on self-proclaimed "long weekends." I maintained a 4.0 GPA, traveled and performed with the Dunk Team, and secured a coveted practice spot with Cosmo the Cougar.

Even though I was more successful than I ever had been before, I stopped writing in my journal. I considered myself a failure just because I was gay. I was embarrassed by the thought of someone one day reading it only to realize what a disappointment I was. I defined my entire life by the one thing I couldn't seem to get right. I didn't see the man that aced exams, backpacked hundreds of miles, and did flips off railings. I saw only the boy that couldn't sleep at night, doubted his beliefs, and cowered at the thought of an ambiguous future.

My cousin Rachel's words when I came out to her the following year meant more than she will ever know: "This doesn't define you." In that moment, she helped me realize that I am more than my sexual orientation. Rachel had me take a step back and see myself for who I truly am, not just for the one aspect of myself I didn't like. I've since learned that a healthy perspective for me is to appreciate and honor that I'm gay but not to obsess over it. Rather than give excessive weight to certain parts of who I am, I seek for balance. My life is fuller when others see me—and when I see myself—as a whole picture.

Being gay has greatly influenced who I am, but I am so much more than just gay. I am a son, a brother, an uncle, and a friend. I am an athlete, a dancer, a writer, and an extrovert. There are a multitude of labels and characteristics I use to describe myself. I've identified myself by where I've lived, the schools I've attended, the church I belong to, and the interests I have. All of these classifications are meaningful and help people catch a glimpse into important parts of my life; they come together to paint a more holistic picture of who I am. Each label is relevant, but they can all be encapsulated in my most important identity—a child of God.

Developing healthy perspectives isn't always easy. Sometimes it means going against thought patterns I have hewn to for years. Stepping back, reframing, and looking at life from new vantage points takes patience and practice, but it has led me to more peace and heightened understanding.

One day I received a phone call from Parker, a friend who was struggling to reconcile his faith with his orientation.

"I feel like I'm being torn apart," he said with a trembling voice. "It's like—like there are two pieces inside of me that are in continual conflict. I'm constantly being pulled in two very different directions. I'm a walking paradox. I hate it. I hate who I am."

I listened quietly.

"I don't know how much longer I can live with my mind, heart, and soul in this constant state of war," he continued through tears.

I paused for a moment and considered the hurt he felt. Hearing my friend talk about himself this way broke my heart. He was unable to see his worth. I knew the magnitude of his feelings—I had spent years with similar thoughts, wondering how long I could last while I felt I was constantly being ripped in two. I don't think there is a gay Christian alive who hasn't felt a similar way. I sat with him in his pain, validated his feelings, and expressed my love and appreciation for who he is.

"Parker," I said after a while, "what if you could reframe the way you see yourself?"

"What do you mean?"

"Yeah, you're a paradox—but what if being a paradox isn't a bad thing?" I continued. "What if you could look at being gay not as a divergence of two worlds, but a convergence?"

"I guess I don't know what you're saying," he replied, sounding puzzled. "How could this possibly be a good thing?"

"Imagine if you could rewrite your dissonance as harmony," I said. "Like yin and yang, two parts of one whole. The forces that you see pulling you apart are *both* important aspects of who you are. Being gay and being a child of God aren't mutually exclusive, because they exist simultaneously in you."

Silence prevailed on the other end of the phone. I could tell my friend was deep in thought.

"I *think* I see what you are trying to say . . . ?" he said finally.

"I wish I knew how to say it better," I replied honestly. "It's so hard to put into words."

Parker then surprised me with an interesting question: "If there were a button that could make you straight, would you press it?"

His inquiry was strikingly similar to a question I had been asked in a podcast interview just a few weeks prior. Both then and now, I knew my answer immediately.

"I feel like pressing the button would irrevocably alter who I am," I said. "If I were straight, I don't think I would be me anymore."

"You wouldn't press it?" he asked for clarification.

"Not a chance."

I shared with Parker some of the impressions I'd received from seeking heavenly guidance concerning my identity. I explained how I feel that for me, being gay is connected to who I am on a much deeper level than what the world sees. I reminded him that a same-gender orientation isn't embarrassing, and has nothing to do with sin or sexual activity. I told him how the two seemingly opposite, contrary forces inside me often feel complementary and interconnected. I explained how, over time, I have seen great blessings that have stemmed from me being gay.

"Parker, if I had that button, I would destroy it," I said frankly.

"Really?" he asked.

"Yes."

"I believe God created me intentionally," I continued. "I'm not ashamed of who I am, and I trust that God has a plan for me. Besides, gay or straight, I feel the most important thing is that I'm striving to become more like the Savior. I have felt healthier and much closer to Him as I've learned to accept who I am rather than wish I were different."

I'd thought the words before, but I couldn't help but notice how certain and happy I felt as I said them out loud. For me, seeking heavenly guidance and reframing the way I see myself has resulted in a paradigm shift in my happiness. I'm grateful the Spirit has helped me hold on to and honor both parts of who I am, even though the world often suggests they are contradictory.

I used to think I had to pick a side. In my binary mindset, I looked at the intersection of my faith and my orientation as an issue of "good and bad," when in reality it was an issue of "me and me." I let the false idea that there were only two ways to live completely blind my agency and my trust, in both myself and in the Lord. This binary mindset only heightened the sense of division I felt within myself. I was so focused on two different sides that I wasn't able to see the beauty in being a paradox, or the way that being gay and being a faithful child of God can both wholly occupy the same space.

I have been much happier as I've begun to recognize and avoid divisive traps of black-and-white thinking. Holding on to and loving these two important aspects of who I am gives me the ability to be creative and exercise my remarkable, God-given capacity to process complex thoughts and feelings. I stretch myself and grow as I take on uncharted territory. I learn from mistakes, set boundaries, and use the Savior's Atonement to become better than I once was. I feel like that's how life is supposed to be—learning and growing as I go. As I pray for direct guidance on how to honor my orientation, I am slowly discovering more about my relationship with God and His plan for me.

This fresh perspective has allowed me to see miracles that have stemmed from my belonging to both the LDS and the

LGBTQ communities. The outlook I have gained from my standpoint at the convergence of these two worlds has allowed me to bless and serve others in a unique way. Many times I have been able to bridge these two communities that I love and care about.

After I came out publicly in early 2019, I began receiving messages from thousands of people. Closeted, struggling individuals all over the world shared stories of hope and healing. Moms wrote about reconnecting with their children, and local Church leaders told me about their new initiatives to make activities and religious discussions more inclusive to all.

I had one particularly beautiful experience with an extended family member. He had come out to his mom, and they were struggling to reconcile his identity with their faith. They felt they were alone. After learning that I was gay, he asked if he could call me. We talked for a few hours, and it was a healing conversation for us both. There was a certain power and understanding between us: We are both gay, both members of the Church of Jesus Christ, and both share the same ancestry. It was amazing to see how being an "out" gay member of the Church gave me a special opportunity to help my very own family.

In society, popular sentiment often reinforces the false notion that we must pick a side when it comes to LGBTQ and religious issues. Many feel they cannot show love and acceptance to others, or themselves, while still living gospel principles. We have, whether intentionally or not, created two camps, and seem to think everyone must fit completely into one of them. At first glance it seems easier to look at some issues as completely black and white, with no tolerance for gray areas, but what happens when the "gray area" is no longer an idea or issue, but a person? What if the "gray area" is a grandchild, a friend, or a niece or nephew?

Separating "believers" and LGBTQ individuals and allies into two separate camps reminds me of what Christ referred to as putting "new wine into old bottles" (Matthew 9:17). These camps were created when many did not have a proper understanding of what being gay actually is. In the past, it was thought to be a choice, and to many it was directly associated with sex, disease, apostasy, and deviance. Few understood that accepting same-sex orientation is *not* equal to accepting a dangerous lifestyle. Additionally, due to cultural and societal pressures, there weren't many examples of openly gay individuals who held on to their faith.

Thankfully, we now have greater light and knowledge. Being gay is not a choice, and there are active LGBTQ members serving and participating in Church congregations worldwide. However, the idea that there are two competing sides is still very much alive.

Putting our "new wine" of understanding more about our gay brothers and sisters into "old bottles" of binary thinking upholds two separate, distinct groups. When binary thinking is involved, polarization follows, thus deepening any divides. Unity comes when we throw out the adversary's "us vs. them" mentality and realize we are all of the same fold. In a recent address to the students of Brigham Young University, President Ballard urged all to "look beyond the narrow categories that often separate us from each other, and instead focus on higher ends." He stated that judging character through "discrimination, racism, sexism, and other social ills will often impose false identities that keep [others], and us, from progressing."

President Ballard boldly declared, "We are all children of God. That makes us family—brothers and sisters bound by a common divine heritage. That one simple, unifying fact should override all else that we allow to cause separation and division among us. . . . Marginalizing and persecuting people based on age, gender, nationality, religious preferences, or anything else can be hurtful. . . . We must always remember that there are also larger groups to which people belong. . . . For us, the group that is most important to identify with is being the children of God. We declare that we are all the spiritual children of Heavenly Parents. . . . We consider every person divine in origin, nature, and potential. Each possesses seeds of divinity" (BYU devotional, Mar. 3, 2020).

Just before graduating from BYU, I had a humbling conversation with Julie, a high-ranking administrator at the university. She told me about many things she had been involved with in her impressive career. She talked about large-scale initiatives, designing new buildings on campus, and directing a large department. Then, with teary eyes, she said, "Charlie, I want you to know that even with all of those accomplishments, the most meaningful thing I have done in my career is this work with LGBTQ students. You have changed the way I see the world. You have taught me how to love."

Like Julie, many have expressed to me that when they first started venturing into the world of gay issues, they aimed to help people who felt marginalized and cut off. They wanted to be Samaritans to those who were struggling to keep their faith. Many are surprised to find the gay community is actually a blessing to them. By associating with people who don't fit the mold, many have learned how to better show compassion and empathy toward others. They have learned how to be more like the Savior—less othering and more inclusive.

A black-and-white perspective regarding LGBTQ and religious issues leads to division. It led to a division within me, as well as within my friend Parker, who expressed the pain he experienced as he felt forced to pick a side. Binary thinking has led to division among family members, friends, and loved ones all over the world. It has led to division in churches, schools, and entire communities.

Aren't we so done with being divided?

The Savior has given clear instructions on how to ensure that our perspectives are healthy and aligned with truth. Jesus Christ taught, "By their fruits ye shall know them" (Matthew 7:20). Each of us has been given heavenly tools to help us as we reframe and seek healthy perspectives on life. The Light of Christ, the power of prayer, and the gift of the Holy Spirit have all helped me recognize good fruits as I have sought to align my perspective with the Savior's.

When doubts arise, I seek to keep sweet, peaceful moments of assurance alive and active. I remind myself of the beautiful experiences and feelings that have resulted from my new perspective. When comparing my mental, emotional, and spiritual health, I clearly see that I am in a much better place now than I was before. My capacity to show Christlike love toward myself and others has also increased immensely.

When I question the direction I am headed, I think of the advice the Lord gave to Oliver Cowdery, as recorded in the Doctrine and Covenants: "Verily, verily, I say unto you, if you desire a further witness, cast your mind upon the night that you cried unto me in your heart, that you might know concerning the truth of these things. Did I not speak peace to your mind concerning the matter? What greater witness can you have than from God?" (D&C 6:22–23).

When I am weary and feel despair, I remind myself what God taught me when He spoke peace to my mind concerning the matter: God did not create me by mistake. I am not the compound of two parts that cannot exist simultaneously. Instead, I am a beloved child of God, blessed with a unique worldview and spiritual gifts that can help me grow, progress, and serve others as I strive to work through the complexities of life.

My Heavenly Parents' view of who I am is much more comprehensive than my own. Their eternal perspective is able to see how my muddled colors come together to create a full, beautiful picture. By prayerfully widening my perspective, I have come to understand more about myself and who my Heavenly Parents need me to be. I've developed healthier attitudes and learned how to more fully fulfill the measure of my creation. Reframing how I see myself has revealed that I do not have to choose between two integral parts of who I am. The inner conflict that tormented me has been replaced by love and peace.

On a larger scale, by collectively widening our perspectives, we can heed prophetic counsel to create safe spaces where all feel welcome. Like the Monet painting at the Getty, made from different strokes and colors of paint, the kingdom of God is comprised of many different kinds of people. Rather than maintain an environment that fosters estrangement and separation, we can throw out binary thinking and replace it with Christlike love. When we step back and look at the big picture, we might just see how we all come together to create something beautiful.

It just takes a fresh perspective.

13

STANDING ROOM ONLY

WHEN I LEFT the locker room I felt determined to speak up, but I didn't feel as confident the next morning when I arrived outside the athletic director's office. I stared at the doorway and thought about how much I loved being the mascot and studying at BYU. I was terrified that saying anything might put both my passion and my education at risk. I had to remind myself what I had accomplished for the university in the past few weeks—Cosmo's dance video with the Cougarettes seemed to be popping up on every handheld device in the country. *This morning, Cosmo was on the front page of a Dutch newspaper.* I forced the thought. *People everywhere are talking about BYU because of you. You have a strong voice. She will listen,* I said to myself, rather unconvincingly.

If I would have heard the locker-room talk a year earlier, it would have destroyed me. I had become somewhat accustomed to hearing hurtful and improper remarks on campus about gay people. In the past, each time someone would make a careless or cruel remark about the LGBTQ community, I let it push me deeper into hiding. The night before as I was leaving the locker room, however, I realized I deserved a better environment. I thought about other closeted students as well, undoubtedly subject to the same verbal abuse. Many of them didn't have a voice. I felt a solemn duty to speak up.

I said a quick prayer, wiped my palms on the sides of my jeans, and knocked three times on the heavy wooden door.

"Hi! Come in!" said the woman who answered. She was tall—almost as tall as I was. She led me to a chair across from her desk and offered me a mint from the jar on her table. I sat down and mentally rehearsed what I had planned to say. I hoped that somehow, to her, my achievements as Cosmo would make up for the fact that I was gay.

"I'm Liz," she said with a smile. "I'm not sure I recognize you from any of the teams—what sport do you play?"

I briefly introduced myself and revealed my identity as the mascot.

"This is you?" she said with excitement, turning her computer to show me a still frame of my video. "You're amazing! Your dancing has brought a lot of good press to the athletic department. You're very talented."

"Thanks! I really appreciate that," I replied.

We talked a while about what it was like to be Cosmo and how I got the idea to perform with the dance team.

"I wanted to meet with you because I have a few concerns," I finally said. "I love this university—I really do—but I don't always feel safe here."

"How so?" she asked as she intently lowered her chin.

"Well . . . I'm gay," I began. "I dedicate all of my free time and all of my talents to building BYU, but I don't always feel safe here. I . . . I guess I don't feel like I belong."

I recounted the jarring conversation I had overheard in the locker room the night before. I told her about other comments made by students and professors I heard almost every day. I explained how hard it was for me to represent a group of people that consistently devalued a core part of me.

"I give everything I have to positively represent BYU, but I can't see how BYU positively represents me. I don't know of any resources for gay students on campus. There isn't any visible support or acceptance either," I continued. "If I'm being honest, I can handle the comments. I can handle the slurs. They hurt, but I'm at the point where I'm confident enough that they don't bother me as much anymore. What I can't handle is the thought of students all over this campus who are still struggling. It crushes me to know there are students who feel like I used to, who have to hear things like this every day. People act like we don't even exist. It's not safe. It's not sustainable," I finished.

I looked up at her expectantly, trying to read the emotions on her face.

"Thank you for sharing this with me," she said. "It takes a lot of courage."

She turned around and grabbed a framed quote from a shelf behind her.

"I was gifted this by a friend last week. It's from Encircle, a local LGBTQ nonprofit organization that started up last year. Have you heard about it?"

I nodded my head.

"I'm a really big fan of their slogan: 'No Sides, Only Love,'" she said. "I know this is a big issue on campus. For the past year I've been assigned to address it."

"Really?" I asked in disbelief.

"Yes. I've become quite passionate about it too."

She expressed her desire to build bridges and find common ground among students and professors regarding LGBTQ issues. She asked me follow-up questions about my campus experience and didn't judge, diminish, or make any assumptions about me. She told me everything BYU was already doing to try to foster more unity on campus and reported on an NCAA training seminar she had recently attended.

"It's pretty cool that I chose you to talk to about this, huh? I had no idea you were in charge of advocacy efforts," I said. Our long conversation was coming to a close.

"I don't think it's a coincidence," she said assuredly. "I've been looking for an LGBTQ student-athlete. I'm sure there are more than just you, but nobody is 'out.'"

"That doesn't surprise me," I said, halfway between a sigh and a laugh.

"We might be able to use your help . . ."

Five months later, I stood in an empty auditorium, hopeful but not expectant. Ever since meeting with Liz, my life had been a complete whirlwind. I was busier than ever with Cosmo appearances. I spent almost every weekend out of town with mascot gigs and events. Schoolwork was slipping away. I fought to keep my GPA high, always hurriedly voice-recording my notes so I could listen to them at double speed while driving to and from work. But even with all the time demands of Cosmo, Dunk Team, work, and school, I gladly let my new responsibilities consume any free moment I could find.

Liz helped assign me to a working group with a few university administrators and other LGBTQ students. We spent hours together, writing charters, finalizing proposals, and brainstorming ideas on how we could make campus safer for marginalized students. I didn't know how passionate I was about the cause until I was knee-deep in it. Every breakthrough or victory felt like winning a marathon. Every setback or disappointment felt like losing a piece of my heart.

Today was make it or break it. For the first time ever, the university had given permission to hold an LGBTQ-specific event on campus. We had spent weeks planning a question-and-answer panel, hoping to foster empathy and educate students regarding challenges that come with being LGBTQ on campus. We chose four students to represent our group and set up an electronic question submission queue for the moderator. The only real promotions for the event were a few posters that hung around campus, and the success of this panel would determine the longevity of our working group.

"Hey, bro, you nervous?" my brother Sam asked when he walked into the room.

"Yeah, really nervous, and I'm not even on the panel," I replied. I had stayed completely behind the scenes the entire time I was volunteering. The only people who even knew I was an ally were the other members of the working group.

"How many people are you expecting?" he asked.

"I have no idea," I replied honestly. "Part of me thinks a lot, but then again, maybe people won't care as much as I hope."

My dad and little sister Hannah walked in. She was still in high school, but they happened to be in town for a university tour.

"Hey!" I said. "Uh . . . you guys aren't technically supposed to be here. It's for students only. I mean, I'm really happy to see you, but I don't want to cross anyone . . ."

"Yeah, right," my dad said with a laugh. "You think we'd miss your big day?"

"You've been working on this for months, Charlie. There's no way we'd sit it out!" said Hannah enthusiastically.

"I'm not even doing anything, though! I'm only comfortable behind the scenes," I replied, feeling grateful but slightly embarrassed.

"We're proud of you either way. I'm not leaving even if they try to drag me out," Dad said.

"Same," Hannah agreed.

The three of them took a seat on the back row while I went to my spot at the front of the room. Little by little students began to arrive.

"Five minutes," said one of the students from the working group. "I'd say this is a pretty fair turnout. About what I expected."

I looked around. So far there were about two hundred students in the auditorium.

"I wonder how many more will come?" I ventured.

"We'll see. I don't know how popular it is to support gay students on campus, though," she replied.

I thought about the guys in the locker room a few months before and what they had said about people like "us."

"You ready?" Liz asked as she walked in. Huge groups of students were piling in behind her.

"Ready as we'll ever be," said my friend Ben, one of the guys who was on the panel.

"Awesome," she answered, and then she turned to me. "Charlie, would you be comfortable offering a closing prayer afterwards?" she asked.

My heart started beating faster. More and more people were filing into the room. I looked around and saw many familiar faces—friends from business classes, old freshman hallmates, and a few of the girls on the cheer squad. We were approaching maximum capacity, and I could hear people around me hurriedly making plans to designate overflow rooms for a live stream. Could I really stand up and pray at an event like *this* in front of so many of my peers?

"I don't know," I said honestly.

"No worries. If you do feel comfortable by the time things are wrapping up, you can get up to say the prayer. If not, shoot me a look and I'll do it instead," she offered.

"Sounds good," I replied sheepishly.

By the time the panel began, the room was absolutely packed. Every seat was filled, and students were sitting on the floor and standing in the aisles. I got a text from another member of the working group, who said two overflow rooms were filling up fast.

I sat next to the computer and helped monitor questions that were being submitted to the online queue. Many of them were expected: "When did you know you were gay?" "How do you reconcile who you are with your beliefs?" Others caught me off-guard: "How can I be an ally to my LGBTQ brothers and sisters?" "What can I do to make campus a safer place for gay students?"

I had no idea there was this much support at BYU.

The Spirit burned strong as the panelists bore testimonies of their divine creation. I could almost feel hearts being softened as they shared experiences and cleared up common misconceptions.

"I often get asked what made me gay," said Ben into the microphone. "During my time as an undergrad I went to the BYU library and read a few books on what causes same-sex attraction. I read about overbearing mothers and distanced fathers, early sexual trauma, and not connecting with my masculinity. None of these made any sense in my life. I started to realize that my sexuality is one ingredient that makes up who I am. Just like my religion, my profession, my hobbies, and my relationships, my sexuality isn't something that happened to me; it's part of me. It's part of the way I was created by loving Heavenly Parents."

I listened to Ben give powerful answers and wished that one day I could be that brave. I had come a long way in the past year, but I wasn't sure I would ever be courageous enough to be as open and vulnerable as he was—I still wasn't even sure if I could say the closing prayer. I looked around at faces of people in the crowd. Some were smiling brightly, beaming with optimism and hope. Others were teary-eyed, overcome with the love and emotion that permeated the room. In the very back I saw my family. Never in my wildest dreams did I think they would support me in something like this, but here they were, adamantly breaking the rules just to show me how much I was loved.

The scene was a stark contrast to the locker-room conversations and awkward class discussions I had witnessed before. I had spent every day for the past few years feeling paranoid and alone on campus, but I now realized there were allies I had never known existed. I felt humbled to be part of the group that had made such support visible. After the last question was answered, Liz looked at me from across the room, trying to read my body language. I thought for a few moments about the crowd behind me, then gave a confident nod. I didn't feel nerves, anxiety, or hesitation when I stood up from my seat. I felt only love.

I walked behind the podium, raised the microphone to my mouth, folded my arms, and began to pray.

14

THE NORMS

OUT OF ALL the friend groups at Willard High School, the "Norms" were, without a doubt, the coolest. The group consisted of my two older sisters and a few of their closest friends. I was a few years younger, but the Norms always made me feel valued and important. Sometimes they all came over to get ready for parties or events. I would watch them put on makeup and help pick out what to wear. After graduation they took a senior trip to the beach with my family and I got to tag along. They didn't complain that a nerdy middle-schooler was following them around. Instead, they invited me to dinners, raced with me on the sand, and designated me their official trip photographer.

The Norms were all beautiful and talented, but what made them awe-inspiring was the way each of them was true to who they were.

"Whoa, whoa, whoa. Where are you going?" my mom would ask my older sisters as they were throwing on mascara and running out the door.

"To a party," Anne would say nonchalantly.

My mom's quizzical expression would shift to a look of hesitation and concern.

"With the Norms!" Janine would add.

"Oh!" my mom would reply, the trust and relief evident in her voice. "Have fun! Tell them all I say hi!"

My sisters and some of their friends created the Norms their freshman year when they realized peer pressure and poor decisions were rampant at school. They decided early on to stick together, thereby ensuring none of them ever felt pressured to make decisions contrary to their personal goals or beliefs. The Norms weren't an official crew, just a group of sincere, trustworthy girls who wanted to be comfortable and make good choices. While the group name originally referred to the tight-knit friends that "normally" hung out together, over time it grew to represent a group of young women so confident in who they were that they set the new "norm" of what others aspired to be. By the time senior year rolled around, the Norms were the most popular girls in school. Everyone wanted to be a Norm.

My sisters and their friends understood they didn't have to submit to their surrounding culture in order to fit in. Instead, they created their own culture, which allowed them to be comfortable and to thrive, no matter their environment. They built a reliable friend group based on shared values and trust, allowing them to actively create safety for themselves. They were authentic, and they successfully carved out their own paths, even when it proved challenging.

I realized a desperate need for my own "Norms" when I was on the cusp of coming out and struggling to find a place to fit. I felt awkward and out of place at church, like I was on the outside looking in. I wondered if I would feel more at home in social circles where everyone was openly gay.

One day I decided to go to a gay social gathering. I didn't know anyone who was going to be there, but I was confident in my ability to step out of my comfort zone and make new friends. Upon arrival, I realized the enjoyable gathering I had anticipated was actually a wild party. I walked around uncomfortably, feeling like a fish out of water. Within minutes I was pressured by multiple people to make choices that went against my personal values. They mocked and berated me when I politely declined. I left almost immediately, feeling angry, disappointed, and alone. On the drive home I felt prompted to call a friend. He was gay too, and I figured he might have experienced similar frustrations.

"I don't get it," I ranted. "These are supposed to my people. Shouldn't they understand where I come from and who I am? They were horrible to me. Why would they make fun of me for staying true to myself?" I said. "And how can anyone expect to find safety and community in an environment that swarms with addictive substances and immorality?"

My friend listened carefully to my questions and concerns. "Sometimes hurt people hurt people," he replied, "and a lot of people in the gay community have been hurt. Most of us have been raised to believe we are deviants, so that's—well, that's kind of what some of us become. It's almost like self-fulfilling prophecy."

He continued, "When people strip you of your confidence and self-worth like that, it's easy to turn to destructive habits as a way to numb the pain. Then that almost becomes the expectation."

What he said made sense.

"You know, though, just because you have the same orientation as someone doesn't automatically make them your kind of person," he said wisely. "You have being gay in common with these guys, but that doesn't mean you necessarily have the same interests or goals."

"You're right," I agreed. "Ugh, I feel so stupid!"

"You're not stupid. I learned that lesson the hard way too."

He explained to me how being true to himself after coming out had often resulted in going against the grain.

"There are some things about gay culture that I really like," he said. "Others I really don't, and I'm okay with that. It doesn't always make me popular, but I'd rather be authentic than pretend to be someone I'm not. Why did you go to the party alone?" he added unexpectedly.

"I don't have anyone to go with," I answered.

"Is that really true?"

I thought about it. "Yeah. It is. I'm too gay for the Mormons and too Mormon for the gays," I finally said, exasperated. "I don't fit in either group."

"Maybe on the surface that's true," he continued, "but I'm sure there are plenty of people who wouldn't label you as either, and would just see you as Charlie. Why don't you focus on creating your own tribe, where you can be yourself? Find people who care about you—people who honor your value system and personal goals. Then, next time you're in a situation like this—and there will undoubtedly be a next time—you'll have someone that can come with you."

I realized I was operating in uncharted territory without a solid support system. Most everyone I was "out" to lived far away, and I was unconsciously supporting the false idea that I had to separate my friend groups based on religion and sexual orientation. My friend had a good point: Until I had a support system, I would probably always feel fractured and alone. I needed to create my own tribe so I could have solid support no matter where I was.

As I had done with my family, I came out to the remainder of my friends in a prayerful, calculated way. I expressed my desire for support as I worked through the challenges I was facing. Many of them reacted the same way my brother had, by asking a few questions, expressing trust in my decisions, and stating nothing would change. In most cases, coming out to my friends strengthened our relationships.

I created my own "Norms" with a mix of true friends who share similar interests and values. Some are former college teammates; others are friends from my hometown. Some are professional consultants or dancers; others are students or aspiring artists. They are diverse in every way—a mix of straight, gay, male, female, religious, nonreligious, old, and young—but all of them have my back, no matter what. Whenever I need support, I know where I can turn. Like my sisters, I have actively been able to create a safe environment wherever I am. When a situation is unfamiliar or uncomfortable, I can call on any one of my "Norms" to go with me.

My "Norms" have also shown me I don't have to fall into one of the two cultural grooves that dominate the gay LDS experience. In the years I have spent watching people, I've noticed that polarization between gay and religious cultures often creates a vacuum in which people feel forced to pick a side. Looking at the two most common trends leads me to feel disheartened and overwhelmed. They have historically resulted in either physical or spiritual death.

Within conservative organized religions, LGBTQ members are dying. I've watched for years as individuals have become anxious, depressed, and suicidal as they've doubled down on themselves and lied about who they are. Many were taught they could change themselves through prayer or conversion therapy, and—like I was—are devastated when it doesn't work. Others have been met with very real challenges as they have tried to homogenize with church culture. I once had a heart-crushing conversation with someone who was contemplating taking her own life.

"If I were dead, I wouldn't have to deal with this conflict," she said. "If I were dead, I could finally have a place where I belong."

In a deep conversation with another friend, I carefully asked if he could identify any root catalysts for his suicide attempt. He told me a local church leader had counseled that he would be "fixed" by the Resurrection after he died.

"I wanted to kill myself because I was told I would be straight in heaven," my friend said to me with distant eyes.

The words, attitudes, and actions sometimes found within well-meaning religious cultures can have extremely negative psychological effects on gay individuals. When combined with a stark lack of healthy role models or visible support systems, they feel marginalized. The suicide rate among LGBTQ youth in conservative Christian religions is markedly higher than the national average. We must do better.

Another alarming pattern is evident in many who renounce organized religion. I've seen countless individuals who have reacted to emotional trauma with a pendulum swing in their moral values. They "free" themselves from the "cage" of religion, but immediately fall into other traps. I saw this for the first time when I went to the wild gay party. There are many hurting souls who turn to unhealthy coping mechanisms as a way to escape their heartache, which in time results in a form of spiritual death. I've observed that gay culture is so full of substance abuse, addiction, and casual immorality in part because so many heartbroken people are just looking for a place to fit in.

The truth is, cultures aren't cut-and-dried. No one can be perfectly defined by generalizations about a group with whom they associate. When I tried to force myself to fit within predominant Church culture, I felt sad. When I looked to gay culture for a place to fit, I was disappointed to find immorality, drug abuse, and the expectation to lower my standards. I saw heartbreak and loneliness on both sides. Even though I belong to both groups, I usually felt too gay to fit in with Church members and too "churchy" to fit in with gays.

The happiest LGBTQ people I know belong to a third group—valiant individuals who are faithful to who they are and to what they know to be true, no matter what cultural expectations tell them. They understand that heavenly guidance comes when they actively seek connection with God.

I used to laugh at a cheesy motivational poster that hung in my elementary school hallway. It showed a school of gray fish swimming downward, packed tightly together. Within the mass of gray fish was a singular orange fish swimming in the opposite direction. The lone fish was smaller than the rest, but its strikingly bright color made it easily stand out. Underneath the picture was a bold caption that said, "Be true to who you are."

As fate would have it, years later I feel a lot like that little orange fish. As I swim against some of the cultural currents within my church and the gay community, I often feel like the odd fish out. Being a gay member of The Church of Jesus Christ of Latter-day Saints, I'm not always popular as I try to be myself and follow God's plan for me. When I feel threatened or misunderstood by others, I try to remember a piece of funny advice my little sister Hannah gave me: "All the greats have haters, Charlie. The fact that people get ruffled just means you are doing something different." Hannah's motto reminds me that I'm happiest when I am living how I feel called to live, and it's okay when my path looks different. According to her, being different makes me great.

2 Nephi 2:26 teaches that by the redemption of Christ, all are free to act for themselves, not to be acted upon. The gift of agency means we can create our own personal culture. I find

comfort knowing I don't have to wholly subscribe to an existing mold. Instead, I can carve my own path—one that feels true to who I am, and who God created me to be.

Part of acting and not being acted upon means checking where I'm at and where I'm headed. Like using a GPS system in traffic, I constantly seek to reassess my life and check if there are any alternative routes I should take. I prayerfully ask myself:

- Why am I doing what I'm doing?
- Am I evaluating my decisions based on my personal values?
- What are the underlying causes of my actions and feelings?
- Am I seeking personal revelation as I make decisions?
- Am I making any snap decisions because I'm trying to feel numb or run away from an emotion?
- Are there any creative or credible options I haven't considered?
- Am I happy with the direction I am headed?
- Do I feel I'm where God needs me to be?

Such introspection has helped me carve a path based on my own spiritual value system, not a preset cultural mold.

The greatest example of one who broke a preset mold is the Savior. Jesus Christ came into the world at a time of division and polarization. The Jewish world was torn between Greek and traditional thought, and believers often separated themselves among Pharisees, Sadducees, and Essenes. Each Jewish subculture had different viewpoints on truth and acceptable behavior. The Savior never assimilated into an existing side. Tempting as it may have been, Jesus never changed who He was to appeal to any one group, but always stayed true to God (see Hebrews 10:7). He treated all equally and transcended barriers by carving a new path. He taught that Church culture isn't always God's culture, and fulfilled the sacred, individual work that He alone was sent to earth to complete.

During His short three-year ministry, Jesus flipped the existing way of life and created a new standard of empathy and love. Even in the face of extreme conflict and adversity from His own people, Christ was true to Himself and to His divine purpose. In short, He was authentic. I believe that, as children of God, we become more Christlike when we elevate ourselves above cultural classifications and become authentic like Jesus, true to ourselves and to what we believe. My ultimate goal is to become more like the Savior. I pray I can always live authentically, fully accepting who I am while continuously striving to do the will of the Father.

My sisters' example taught me that being authentic within an established culture sometimes comes at the cost of carving a new path, but honoring oneself is always worth it in the end. They never let other people dictate their actions, and they thrived nonetheless. The Norms were more than cultural byproducts, and they grew to be visible role models of healthy, happy lives. Others saw their light and were better because of it. Just like the Norms, when we live authentically, we can create new cultures that foster success.

I've never felt right when I've tried to fit in by abandoning parts of who I am. I thrive when I'm true to myself and to what I believe, regardless of what others might think.

15

MANY THE MILES

"WE'LL HAVE TO push our next meeting back until later tonight," said the man through his thick Middle-Eastern accent. "You two can head back to your hotel and sleep for a while; I'm sure you're tired from your long journey."

We had arrived in Cairo just a few hours before. I didn't know if I had ever been so tired in my life, but the last thing I wanted to do in Egypt was lie around in a hotel room all day.

"Thank you," my dad responded cordially. "We will get some rest and see you tonight."

At first I was surprised by his response, but as they shook hands, my dad gave me his signature look, and I understood that we wouldn't be going back to the hotel room to rest. The next thing I knew, we were driving down a crowded interstate, weaving through cars and potholes and dodging the occasional pedestrian.

Cairo sprawled all around us, seemingly without end. Dust whipped through the dry air and shook the bright, hanging leaves of desert palms. Stucco buildings rose like Jenga blocks in every direction, decorated with vibrant, wet cloth left out to dry in the hot sun. The streets were crowded, colorful, and chaotic. People walked confidently through traffic, dressed in flowing robes and checkered turbans. Donkeys pulled brightly painted wooden carts through side alleys and crowds, and vendors sold desert fruit on roadside stands. The Nile River daringly cut through the city like a wide vein of silver, and in the distance stood the Great Pyramids of Giza, solemn giants overlooking the grandeur of the ancient world.

The endless city came to a startling halt where the pyramids marked the beginning of the Sahara Desert. I had always dreamed of one day seeing them with my own eyes, but never fully believed I would. I touched their smooth, carved limestone and marveled at the history they held. I did flips in the hot desert sand, and my dad took pictures of me soaring through the air with their broad silhouettes in the background. For the past year I had been teaching him about light, angles, and photography, and student met master when he snapped a perfectly set picture of me on a camel in front of the pyramids.

The day reminded me of when I used to work with my dad when I was younger, when we would swim in the river, follow cougar tracks, or hike the bluffs overlooking our land in between feeding cattle. He always had a way of weaving life lessons and adventure into work. We had come to Egypt for business, but true to the Bird way, we found time to explore ancient buildings, climb sand dunes, and ride camels through the open desert. My dad took me to historical markers and museums packed with remarkably intricate hieroglyphics, perfectly preserved mummies, ancient jewelry, and precious golden artifacts. In the evening we sat on the edge of the Nile and watched the sun begin to set over the light-blue Arabian sky.

We barely made it back to our meeting in time. I rushed to prepare my computer, then sat down with a yawn. Moments later

I connected to a hotspot and opened my phone to dozens of messages from friends and family.

"Ding. Ding. Ding. Ding. Ding." I quickly switched it to vibrate.

"Dad, look at this . . ." I whispered, showing him my phone under the table. We stared at a news article with a huge picture of me at the top: "Guest opinion: Everyone loved me as Cosmo the Cougar, but would they love who I was behind the mask?"

"Whoa. They actually published it," Dad said.

Over the past two months we had brainstormed ideas and gone over at least a dozen different drafts. I knew the article was going to be released, but I didn't expect it to be so soon. I almost couldn't believe I had submitted it—in the past I never would have had the courage to come out so openly. Now the whole world knew I was gay, and there was no going back.

Cigar smoke swirled through the air and filled the dim room with a sweet, acrid smell. Sugar cubes made clinking sounds against glass as businessmen dropped them into their Arabic tea. BYU, Cosmo, and my article were a world away. *This is so weird,* I thought as I tried to focus. *My life is exploding right now, and I'm on the opposite side of the globe.*

Throughout the meeting I caught myself staring at a big, round analog clock that hung above the conference table. Its hands moved slowly around roman numerals. After what seemed like an eternity, the conversation faded and the chairs were scooted out from the table. Our red-eye flight left in just over an hour, so I fought the urge to take out my phone and reread the article, and instead we hurriedly grabbed our things and rushed to the airport.

By the time we landed at JFK, my Cosmo coming-out article was the #1 trending story in Utah and was breaking into news stations all across the U.S. I took my phone off airplane mode and was shocked to see thousands of message requests from everyone from grateful LGBTQ youth, to parents, to news reporters.

"Dad . . . my article . . ." I beamed. "People want to interview me," I said excitedly as we walked off the plane into the airport terminal. "Like, a lot of people," I added as I scrolled. "That's pretty cool, huh!"

"Go to Salt Lake," he said casually, almost without thinking.

"What?"

"Go to Salt Lake," he repeated.

"Dad . . . I can't just up and go to Salt Lake. We just got back, and I have a lot to do."

"Charlie, you have been trying to find a way to put yourself out there and help people for over a year, and now you have a big opportunity. Don't let this pass."

What he said made sense, but the idea still seemed crazy. I couldn't just go to Salt Lake. I was in Egypt this morning. And now I was in New York. Salt Lake was still two thousand miles away.

"You felt called to do this, right?"

"Yes," I replied.

"Then get on the next flight and go."

"What about work?" I asked.

"It seems like you have a more important job right now," he replied.

I looked at him and tried to read his face. In the past year my dad had become my biggest support. He didn't particularly like my church, but he was passionate about helping me find a path where I could keep my faith and live a happy, authentic life. He was invested in my desire to help other gay members of the Church as well.

"Charlie. Go."

"Okay," I said in disbelief before heading to check for available tickets. "Thanks, Dad. I love you."

Not too long before that, a relationship like this with my dad had seemed altogether impossible. Just over a year before, I was in the very same airport terminal on my way to visit him for the 2018 New Year's holiday. He had been in Missouri the week before, and I had been cold and distant the whole time we were together. He must have sensed something was off, because as soon as he returned to his place in New York, he called me and asked if I wanted to come visit him for New Year's Eve. While on the plane I took out my laptop and typed out my New Year's goals. My first resolution was to come out to him, though I wasn't sure it was possible. There was a reason he was my only immediate family member who didn't know—there was nothing more terrifying to me than telling my dad I was gay.

My dad's distaste for gay people was majorly impacted by his upbringing. His exposure to sexual minorities in rural Missouri had been limited, so his views were constructed only by what he had learned from society and from Church leaders. He had been steeped in a culture of prejudice since he was a child, and he thought being gay was loud and embarrassing. He thought people chose their orientation and was taught that openly gay people pose a threat to society. My dad's social views were evident in the language he used when talking about any man who was gay, or who he considered too feminine. He didn't like gay people, but he loved to make fun of them.

From early childhood I was hyper-aware of his views. Every derogatory comment he had ever made was burned into my brain. When men sat too close or had emotional relationships, he mocked them. If anyone had interests or qualities that weren't considered stereotypically masculine, he expressed distaste through emasculating jokes and harsh homophobic slurs. My dad's attitudes toward gay people had left me with years of emotional damage and pain, and lately, that pain had caused me to distance myself from him. He had instilled in me the idea that gay people were second-class citizens, making me feel even more ashamed of myself than I already was.

As I grew more confident in my orientation, I felt increasingly angry toward him. I felt like we were in some sort of a split relationship. We could still have fun together and connect on things we had in common, but his homophobic rhetoric was beginning to overpower all of the good things about our relationship. Talking about girls and dating with him was horrible. I hated having to lie and constantly be on my guard every time I was around him. Every comment he made about gay people killed me inside. How could he be so out of touch that he couldn't see what he was doing to me? Was he doing it on purpose?

I hated thinking about how he had forced me into sports and activities he felt were more manly, even though it was obvious my interests were elsewhere. I felt bitter for every time he had made me feel insignificant, worthless, or small, whether intentionally or not. I hated that no matter what I did, I never felt I was good enough for him. There were so many parts of me that didn't fit his expectation of what a man should be. I hated feeling like my identity would keep me from ever truly earning his love and respect.

But above all this, I hated being filled with so much hate. I didn't want to be bitter toward someone I loved so much, even if I had a good reason. Many of my favorite personality traits had come directly from my dad. He had always been charismatic, fun, and adventurous. He taught me how to be strong, capable, and innovative. He showed me by example how to work hard, and how to have fun.

When I was a kid we were best friends. We would spend hours together on the tractor, mowing hay and having competitions to see who could name the most types of fish. I shared with him my big dreams, and he assured me there was nothing in the world that could keep me from accomplishing them. I needed that part of our relationship back—the unconditional love and trust we used to have when I was a child.

I had to tell him I was gay.

The next evening we sat across from each other at a restaurant in Midtown. I scanned the menu for the cheapest item, since I knew I probably wouldn't be able to eat much. My stomach curled in on itself. I originally hadn't planned on telling him so soon, but this was the last time we would see each other for at least four months. Plus, I had already told enough people that I would soon lose control of who knew. I wouldn't be able to hold on to my secret much longer.

As our food arrived, my thoughts were running at breakneck speed: *How will he react?* I wondered. *Whatever happens, at least I will be in a different position than where I am now, right? Besides, what could he possibly say that's worse than what I've already heard from him?*

A familiar feeling sunk into my stomach. I knew the Spirit was prompting me to come out to my dad here and now, so against my own judgment, I decided to trust God and do it.

Right as I began to open my mouth, a waiter led a couple to the table across from us. My dad looked over at the two men and watched them take their seats.

"Hey, look, do you think those guys are gay?" he sneered.

Is this really happening? I thought. I wanted to disappear.

"Yeah . . . I mean . . . probably. We're in Manhattan, Dad," I replied, trying not to sound too provoked. "I'm going to wash my hands," I said with a jolt, and before he could respond, I got up and headed toward the bathroom.

Once there I locked the door and knelt down shakily by the sink, unbothered by the filthy, water-splattered floor beneath me.

"Heavenly Father?" I began. "Up until now I have always come out when I've felt prompted. I know I felt that prompting, but . . . is this really the right time? Am I really supposed to come out to Dad right now?" I choked.

Something made me pause to open my eyes. I looked down and saw my hands laced together, gently resting on my knees. It struck me that just over six months before, I had been in this same position—in the Washington D.C. Temple, desperate, unsettled, and scared to come out to my Father. The soft cream carpet was now replaced by a dingy tile floor, and my dad wasn't exactly as omnipresent as the Creator of the universe, but the emotional similarities were staggering. I felt a rush of warmth inside me, momentarily sweeping away the uneasiness I felt. I quietly finished my prayer, then walked back into the open restaurant with new determination.

Maybe I can steer the conversation in the right direction? Then it might be easier to bring it up, I thought to myself as I sat back down at the table.

I tried hard, but couldn't find any openings. The sound of clattering forks and chattering strangers made it difficult to focus. As the minutes dragged on, my faith began to dwindle. There didn't seem to be any smooth way to launch into telling my homophobic father that his son was gay. His frequent glances at the couple beside us proved a constant reminder of who I was and the seemingly impossible situation I was in.

"Are you feeling all right?" my dad asked when the waiter took away my untouched spaghetti. "You didn't eat anything, and

I feel like I've been doing all the talking . . . Maybe we should take a taxi home?" he suggested.

"No, I'm fine," I lied. "I want to walk," I followed up earnestly.

"It's freezing outside, and you seem like you're getting sick."

"I feel fine. Let's walk," I insisted.

We started out the door into the sharp winter air. The city was unusually quiet. The bitter cold was anything but inviting, and everyone seemed to have turned in early to recover from New Year's Eve the night before. We walked in silence for three blocks as I tried to put my words together. I felt like a kid again, standing afraid at the top of the high dive.

Okay, I said to myself, taking a deep breath. *I'll just have to bite the bullet and jump.*

"Dad . . . I'm gay," I blurted as we rounded the corner onto Lexington Avenue.

"Huh?" he replied, startled. He slowed his pace.

"You heard me," I said simply.

He stopped walking and looked my direction. He seemed to look past me, his eyes narrow and confused.

"Is this some sort of joke?" he asked.

"Why would I joke about this?" I said, fighting the desperation in my voice.

He began walking again, seemingly emotionless. His pace was even, but his mind seemed to be jumping all over the place as he tried to process how to react. I walked alongside him, looking straight ahead at the sidewalk in front of us. He started talking, but I wasn't sure what he was trying to say. Then, he started to yell.

It was like the news had completely shut him down—he didn't know what to do with it, so he just started yelling. He shouted in agony and cursed at the nameless buildings around us. I felt awkward and numb, my own inability to process the situation making me highly uncomfortable as we walked up the street. It was excruciating.

This was a mistake, I thought. *I never should have told him.*

I frantically began forming an escape plan. I considered running away for the night, then lying low until I could catch my flight home later the next day. I could probably even get a hotel if I needed to. I had my phone and my wallet; my suitcase and personal belongings could just stay in his apartment.

It wasn't a great plan, but anything seemed better than enduring this.

Suddenly my dad stopped in his tracks. He grabbed me by my left shoulder and whipped me around to pull me face-to-face with him. His fingers squeezed tight into my collarbone, causing my body to cave in around my chest. I looked through him, terrified and unable to meet his gaze. His reaction and intentions were all so unclear to me. I held my ground, but stared blankly at the bricks behind him. I didn't know it was possible to feel so brave, yet so small.

"You couldn't tell me," he cracked.

I shifted my vision to stare back at him. I didn't know what to say. His deep green eyes began to well with tears.

"I'm your dad and you . . . you couldn't tell me."

"No . . . How could I?" I said quietly.

I've seen my dad get kicked dozens of times while working cattle. I've seen him stitch his own leg with a needle and thread. I've watched him go through a divorce, mourn the loss of loved ones, and lose everything he's ever worked for; but never until that moment had I seen my dad cry.

There, standing on the corner of Lexington Avenue and 59th Street, my dad wrapped me in his arms and wept.

We walked to his small studio apartment a few minutes later

and began to talk through everything I had never been able to say. He asked me questions about my experiences, and I told him everything I could—openly and honestly. We worked through the pain both of us were experiencing—mine old and bitter, his fresh and full of regret. I watched him harrow in agony as he came to understand the ways he had hurt me through his words and actions, and I realized I had attributed to malice what should have been attributed to ignorance. He explained to me that he didn't understand the collateral damage caused each time he made an offhand comment about gay people; he just didn't know any better. He humbly asked forgiveness for not having the resources, background, or information to do better.

"I was in elementary school at the height of the Cold War," he said as I made myself a peanut butter sandwich to feed the hunger that now roared in my stomach. "In third grade we had emergency drills. Every week our teachers would have us hide under our desks to prepare for an air raid from evil Russians."

I looked at him, somewhat puzzled by the shift in conversation and the beginning of his story.

"The first time I went to Moscow I was expecting to see desolation. I prepared to be met by a dismal city, full of starving, war-obsessed, hateful people. Instead, I found beautiful buildings, world-class restaurants, and people who treated me kindly, even though I was an American foreigner who didn't speak their language. It turns out, a lot of what I had thought about Russians wasn't true."

He continued, "Charlie, you are one of the most remarkable people I have ever known. You have more talent in your pinky finger than most people have in their whole bodies. If you're gay, then everything I believed about being gay must not be true either. If you'll let me, I'll do anything I can to learn your truth, and repair our relationship."

I hopped up to sit on the kitchen counter and considered my reply.

"Dad, it took me twenty-four years to get to where I am," I began.

It was his turn to look puzzled. He wore a careful, hopeful face, seeming to wonder if he had said the right thing.

"It's only fair that I give you that long to figure it out, too," I said matter-of-factly.

His eyes held a promise to not let me down.

"Honestly, you'll probably need it," I added slyly, and we both broke into laughter.

We continued talking until, eventually, the physical and emotional exhaustion of the day wouldn't let us keep our eyes open any longer.

"I love you, Charles," Dad said as he drifted off to sleep. "No more secrets, okay?"

I flipped the light switch and climbed the ladder to my lofted bed.

"I love you too, Dad," I replied. "No more secrets."

The cabin lights were dim as I flew somewhere over the sleepy Midwest. I leaned my shoulder against the side of the plane and turned my head to look out the window at the vast, dark sky beneath me. The steady hum of the engine had put everyone else into a slow, dream-like trance, but I stayed wide awake. I couldn't stop thinking about my dad. Any distance traveled in the past twenty-four hours paled in comparison to how far we had come in our relationship. The man who had mocked and belittled gay people just over a year before was so much different from the one who had just convinced me to hop on a flight to Utah.

It wasn't just my dad who had changed. Emotionally, I was almost unrecognizable compared to my former self. I used to shudder at the thought of anyone knowing I was attracted to men. Now, I was willingly "out" to the entire world. Today marked a new chapter, a turning point where I would share my experiences instead of burying them. I knew the path ahead might be rocky as I began to share my story on a more public scale, but the new uncertainty didn't feel like a weight—it felt more like a life vest.

The magnitude of what "coming out" meant finally hit me. I thought about the years I had spent running away, aching to be somebody else. I looked back on the nights I had passed crumpled in my bed, silently crying out for God to change me. I remembered the mental daggers I had subjected myself to and the layers of shame that had driven me deeper into darkness. I thought about hopelessness, bitterness, pain, and the overwhelming feeling I would never be able to break through to the light.

That was life behind the mask.

Now, I looked toward the future with a hope I hadn't had before. Prayerfully accepting myself helped me see the truth about my identity: Both my faith *and* my orientation are integral to who I am. They are not mutually exclusive, because both exist in me.

As my plane descended and hovered over the runway, I felt nothing but confidence. Through seeking heavenly guidance concerning my identity, I finally allowed God's light to reach me—something I had always known was there but could never seem to find. It was as if God couldn't work through me unless I was willing to truly be me.

And I was ready to be me without the mask.

EPILOGUE

IN MARCH 2019, a few days after my op-ed article was published in the *Deseret News*, I was interviewed by a major news station in Salt Lake City. For over twenty minutes I sat on a wooden stool and answered grilling questions about reconciling faith and sexuality, why I felt the need to come out publicly, and how I deal with challenges as both part of the LGBTQ community and a member of The Church of Jesus Christ of Latter-day Saints. Even the questions about being Cosmo were tricky—I can't spill all the secrets!

When I think back on the interview, for being a freshly "out" twenty-five-year-old amidst the craziest week of my life, I feel like I did a pretty good job.

At least, until the last question:

"So, Charlie Bird, what lies in the future for you? Where do you see yourself ten to fifteen years down the road?"

I probably should have anticipated the question, but somehow it caught me completely off-guard. I gave a lame, generic answer about how in the future, I just always wanted to be "happy and kind" (feel free to look it up on YouTube and cringe). The interviewer wasn't satisfied, so he pushed harder. He asked me what my life decisions would look like socially and culturally. I followed up with a horribly awkward pause and another roundabout answer to buy myself time until the interview was over.

It's a little tragic that I fell flat on my face on live television, but I didn't have an answer. The future seemed too difficult to talk about, because it all felt so uncharted. Since then, I have reflected deeply on who I am and who I want to become. Because I started this project with the goal to make it the book I wish I would have had, I want to take these last few pages to respond to the same interview question, and give the answer I wish I'd had that first week after I came out.

I believe that no matter who we are, or where we have been, we can always reach toward heaven. Each of us is a beloved child of Heavenly Parents, with a Savior who knows us personally. Though my future has a lot of unknowns, I trust that I will find my path as I stay close to God. In ten to fifteen years, I see myself continually following my pattern of seeking heavenly guidance concerning my identity. I see myself memorizing new temples that get built, and making goals to go visit my favorite ones. I see myself using my uninhibited personality to serve others, and being vulnerable with family and friends about my deepest thoughts and struggles.

I see myself speaking to youth groups about the importance of coming to Christ and living in the light. I plan to keep spending Christmas with my family, doing flips in the front yard, and honoring the miraculous birth of my Savior. I plan to be involved with suicide awareness initiatives, and to become a licensed clinical therapist so I can give to others what my therapist gave to me. I plan to continue to love and revere women, but to not try to date them anymore.

Ten to fifteen years down the road, I will continue to be

proactive and prayerful about how to move forward. I will root my decisions in love and faith, not bitterness or fear, and strive to focus on positivity. I see "future me" at Sayre's house eating popcorn and taking notes during general conference. I see a life where I exercise faith and rework my testimony each time it gets damaged by doubt, and continue to study the scriptures, pray often, and renew my baptismal covenants in sacrament meeting each week.

When Cosmo alumni are honored at halftime when I'm thirty-five or forty, I plan on doing a backflip for the crowd at Lavell Edwards Stadium. I'll say it's for old time's sake, but if I'm being honest, I'll probably just do it for the attention. Even as a middle-aged man, I see myself seeking more answers as to what being gay means for me eternally, and how my identities as a gay man and a son of God can both wholly occupy the same space. I see myself advocating for others, and keeping a prayerfully open mind as I seek to reframe the way I see other children of God. I plan to follow the example of Jesus Christ and be authentic to both who I am and what I believe. I will carve my own path, even if it makes me unpopular. No matter where life takes me, I plan to keep the Lord involved in all of my decisions.

I made the difficult decision to come out publicly because of the years I spent believing I was alone. The confusing intersection of faith and sexual orientation is often full of pain, heartbreak, and misunderstanding, and it hasn't yet allowed for many people to share experiences or success stories. I feel grateful for the opportunity to speak openly and contribute parts of my own story. I pray the experiences I have prayerfully chosen to share in this book will build bridges and increase understanding, and never be used to judge, condemn, or place expectations on someone else.

Please use me as a point of reference, not a poster child.

I look to a future where more people understand they don't have to hate themselves to love their church, or hate their church to love themselves. I believe being a faithful disciple of Christ and being gay can go hand in hand. All the while, I hope to see my faith community do better to actively create spaces where all can worship God in a safe, loving environment. If you believe God's LGBTQ children have a place in His Church, please show them where it is. Do your best to walk in their shoes. Please love them and listen to them. Please let them know they are needed. I am confident the Lord will inspire anyone who earnestly desires to help.

Whether it be in ten, fifteen, or even fifty years, I look forward to a future without any masks.

ACKNOWLEDGMENTS

There are a number of people I wish to thank for their influence on *Without the Mask*. If not for Sheri Dew, this book would not exist. She was the catalyst in my decision to write the manuscript and always believed wholeheartedly in this project's ability to uplift and heal. I thank her for openly challenging me and allowing me to challenge her in return. I feel humbled for each opportunity I've had to learn from her. She is not only an inspiring role model but also a sharp businesswoman, a thoughtful ally, and a devoted friend.

Additionally, I feel incredibly grateful I was able to work closely with Laurel Christensen Day, who has been passionate about this project since its inception. Laurel took time to really understand who I am, helped me play to my strengths, and identified important themes to weave throughout the manuscript. Laurel and her team, including Celia Barnes and Tracy Keck, were indispensable to the realization of this project. As one can imagine, publishing this book for its intended audience came with uncertainties and unfamiliar challenges. I don't know of any group who could have represented me better.

I knew publishing this manuscript would take a great deal

of vulnerability. In many ways these words are an extension of myself, and I felt a strong desire to have complete control and ownership of my work. Still, writing this book posed challenges. It was tough separating convoluted thoughts and feelings into logical chapters, and there were multiple stories I found difficult or embarrassing to share. I am very grateful to the numerous individuals who helped me hurdle these challenges as I worked through various drafts.

First and foremost, my parents, my siblings, and each friend named in the book were all crucial to giving feedback and acting as sounding boards. I feel incredibly blessed to have such an invested, selfless, gifted support system. I'm so happy that readers get to catch a glimpse of them through my eyes. Their loyalty and wisdom inspire me.

Many others assisted me with writing and content challenges. Each time I felt stuck, God seemed to provide me with the perfect helpmeet. Molly Finlayson sat on the floor with me to help organize themes from a jumbled mix of thoughts scribbled on index cards. Erin Hart helped me articulate complex emotions when I couldn't write them in a way that made sense (fun fact: she is married to another "former Cosmo"). Delaney Plant helped me bookend my writing and home in on some of the most important sentences of the book. Conversations with friends such as Mitchell Poirier and Katie Jones helped inspire me as I worked on the initial manuscript. Ben Schilaty was among the first to read it in full, and he offered important insights as well as advice on keeping a positive, gospel-centered voice. I greatly value his guidance and feedback.

Finally, I would like to thank Jared Klundt. I would not have had the courage, the strength, nor the emotional intelligence to write this book without him. Jared has been integral to my emotional, mental, and spiritual health, and has done so completely behind the scenes. Before I began writing, I compiled a list of points I wanted to include within the book. Many of them were derived from notes taken from conversations I had with Jared. I am grateful for all he has done for me, and for the LGBTQ community as a whole.

I don't have all the answers yet, but I do know that God loves His children. I felt His guiding hand as I worked to create this book. I am proud of this finished product, and I believe it will not only help keep God's children alive on the earth but also help keep them alive in Christ. I feel humbled and grateful for this entire experience, and hope it opens the door for many more to come.

ABOUT THE AUTHOR

CHARLIE BIRD was Cosmo the Cougar at Brigham Young University from 2016 to 2018. He received national acclaim for his multiple dance performances with the BYU Cougarettes. As Cosmo, he performed on stages across the country, including the ESPN College Football Awards. NBC Sports dubbed 2017–18 the "Year of the Mascot" in honor of Cosmo's character and performance. Charlie was born and raised in southwest Missouri and served a two-year mission for The Church of Jesus Christ of Latter-day Saints in Redlands, California. He graduated from BYU in 2018 with degrees in global supply chain management and Spanish studies, then moved to New York City to work in the global investment and consulting sector. Charlie is an active LGBTQ advocate and is involved with multiple nonprofit LGBTQ organizations across Utah and nationwide. He is currently back in Utah to pursue a master's of social work from BYU in effort to become a licensed clinical therapist.